AF840699

Richard Frimston is a solicitor and consultant with Russell-Cooke LLP in London and former partner and head of their private client group. He advises clients in relation to their estate planning, wills, probate and tax planning issues. He is one of the best-known speakers and writers on the topics of cross border estates and the Regulation.

Jessica Flowerdew is a bi-lingual solicitor and partner with Brodies LLP in Edinburgh. She has particular expertise in UK – French cross border issues and is also a well-known speaker on these topics.

A Practical Guide to the EU Succession Regulation Outside the EU

Second Edition

A Practical Guide to the EU Succession Regulation Outside the EU

Second Edition

The Regulation and its impact on inheritance, and estate administration and planning in the United Kingdom and other third States

Richard Frimston
Solicitor
Russell-Cooke LLP

Jessica Flowerdew
Solicitor
Brodies LLP

Law Brief Publishing

© Richard Frimston and Jessica Flowerdew

All rights reserved. No part of this publication may be reproduced, stored in a retrieval system, or transmitted, in any form or by any means, electronic, mechanical, photocopying, recording or otherwise, without the prior permission of the publisher.

Excerpts from judgments and statutes are Crown copyright. Any Crown Copyright material is reproduced with the permission of the Controller of OPSI and the King's Printer for Scotland. Some quotations may be licensed under the terms of the Open Government Licence (http://www.nationalarchives.gov.uk/doc/open-government-licence/version/3). Any excerpts from EU legislation are reproduced under the terms of the Creative Commons Attribution 4.0 International licence (see https://eur-lex.europa.eu/content/legal-notice/legal-notice.html).

Cover image © iStockphoto.com/AzmanL

The information in this book was believed to be correct at the time of writing. All content is for information purposes only and is not intended as legal advice. No liability is accepted by either the publisher or author for any errors or omissions (whether negligent or not) that it may contain. Professional advice should always be obtained before applying any information to particular circumstances.

Published 2025 by Law Brief Publishing, an imprint of Law Brief Publishing Ltd
30 The Parks
Minehead
Somerset
TA24 8BT

www.lawbriefpublishing.com

Paperback: 978-1-916698-56-7
Hardback: 978-1-918241-00-6

To my wife, Elizabeth, my late daughter
Agnes and my son Edmund.

We will always have Europe.

Mairidh Eòrpa.

PREFACE

As practitioners whose clients have been buying property in France and in other EU Member States since the 1980s, Richard became increasingly interested in the uncertainties and complexities for citizens in cross border succession and estate planning. In 2005 he was asked to join the Commission's expert group that considered the drafting of the Regulation and with the other experts soon discovered how little we knew and how complex was the area of private international law under discussion.

We have been living with the initial Dörner and Lagarde study, the Regulation and the various preliminary drafts and iterations since 2002 and were sad that the UK Government did not feel able to opt in to the Regulation when it was adopted in 2012. The interplay of succession laws in Europe has always been complex and the role of the EU in attempting to simplify matters is also very political. The EU Succession Regulation has been fully effective since the summer of 2015 and has changed the landscape for succession in most of the EU. Misconceptions abound and Brexit has not poured oil on troubled waters. The view of the Regulation from each Member State is individual and different; culture paints the back cloth.

The limitations imposed on the Regulation by changes in France and Germany, have made its application even more complicated and subject to political pressures. Jessica has been following these closely.

This book attempts to look at the subject from the perspective of a practitioner outside the EU, address some of the various topics that may be relevant and attempt to give some answers to the many questions that remain. Virtually every time that we look at the Regulation again, we learn something new. We hope that some of our fascination for the subject and of the things that we have learned on this journey, will be of interest to others.

The world is now changing very rapidly and although the interpretation of the Regulation will continue to change and develop further, the EU institutions may have more pressing matters to concern them. The law is stated as at 31 March 2025.

References in this book to an article or recital in the Regulation are not capitalised, whereas references to Articles or Recitals in other Regulations, Treaties or Conventions are capitalised. Similarly, references to a chapter in this book are not capitalised, whereas references to a Chapter, such as of the Regulation are capitalised.

We are particularly grateful to many European friends over the years and in particular to Dr Timothy Lyons QC and our colleagues Patrick Delas and Christopher Salomons for all of their invaluable help, advice and comments. Any errors are, of course, ours.

Richard Frimston
Jessica Flowerdew
March 2025

CONTENTS

TABLE OF CASES

Siv Ing Benum AS v Kinovox-Benum AB O 743-11 of 31 January 2013 ... 75

Spiliada Maritime Corp v Cansules Ltd [1987] AC 460 ... 30

Taylor v Farrugia [2009] NSWSC 801 ... 207

The Abidin Daver [1984] AC 795 ... 30

T. N. and N. N. v E. G. (on behalf of W.N.), Case C-617/20, Judgment of the Court (Fifth Chamber) of 2 June 2022, ECLI:EU:C:2022:426 … 103, 149-150

Turner v Grovit [2004] WL 5400365 ... 104

Udny v Udny (1869) LR 1 Sc & Div 441, 457 ... 22

UE and HC v Vorarlberger Landes- und Hypotheken-Bank AG, Case C-301/20, Judgment of the Court (Sixth Chamber) of 1 July 2021, ECLI:EU:C:2021:528 … 121

UM v HW (administrator of the estate of ZL), Case C-277/20, Judgment of the Court (First Chamber) of 9 September 2021, ECLI:EU:C:2021:531 … 143, 153, 196

V A and Z A v T P, Case C-645/20, Judgment of the Court (Fifth Chamber) of 7 April 2022, ECLI:EU:C:2022:267 … 76, 100

Villiers v Villiers [2020] UKSC 30 ... 10

W.B. v Notariusz pełniący czynności zastępcy w Krośnie, Case C-658/17, Judgment of the Court (Sixth Chamber) of 23 May 2019, ECLI:EU:C:2019:444 ... 94, 112

W v W [1993] 2IR 476 ... 25

Winkler v Shamoon [2016] EWHC 217 (Ch) ... 63, 152

Yule v Yule (1758) Mor 6400 ... 144

ZVK Zuchtvieh-Kontor GmbH Case C-300/05, Judgment of the Court

TABLE OF OTHER LEGISLATION

Inheritance (Provision for Family and Dependents) Act 1975 ... 83, 169, 206, 207, 221, 226, 228

Inheritance and Trustees' Powers Act 2014 ... 83

Inheritance Tax Act 1984 ... 40, 148, 177, 178

Insolvency Regulation (EC) No. 1346/2000 of 29 May 2000 ... 70, 75, 89, 168

Law of Property Act 1925 ... 130, 131

Maintenance Obligations Regulation (EC) No 4/2009 ... 9, 46, 63, 66, 75

Mental Capacity Act 2005 ... 147

Presumption of Death (Scotland) Act 1977 ... 65

Presumption of Death Act 2013 ... 65

Rome I – Council Regulation (EC) 593/2008 on the law applicable to contractual obligations [2008] OJ L177/6 ... 20, 46, 74, 172

Rome II – Council Regulation (EC) 864/2007 on the law applicable to non-contractual obligations [2007] OJ L199/40 ... 46

Rome III – Council Regulation (EU) No 1259/2010 implementing enhanced cooperation in the area of the law applicable to divorce and legal separation [2012] OJ L/343/10 ... 9, 10, 46

s.23 Wills Act (Manitoba) ... 147

s.37 Wills and Succession Act (Alberta) ... 147

s.58 Will, Estate and Succession Act (British Columbia) ... 147

Succession (Scotland) Act 1964 ... 207

Succession (Scotland) Act 2016 ... 84, 144

Succession Act 1925 (Pakistan) ... 201

CHAPTER ONE

INTRODUCTION

Originally there were six members of European Economic Community ("EEC") which expanded and later became the European Community ("EC").

Since, the accession of Croatia in 2013, and the secession of the United Kingdom on January 31, 2020, there are now 27 Member States ("MS") of the European Union ("EU") in an area of Freedom, Security and Justice with rights of free movement of people, capital, goods and services – the Single Market – with a population of a little under 450 million.

EU institutions

The European Commission is the civil service of the EU that proposes legislation. The Council of the European Union represents the individual member states. The European Union Parliament has members directly elected by citizens in individual constituencies.

Some legislation requires unanimity from the Council of Ministers with no input from the European Parliament, whilst other legislation under what is known as the ordinary legislative procedure requires a majority from the Council of Ministers and a majority from the European Union Parliament.

European Union governments recognised that judicial co-operation was important. Back in 1968, the original six Member States agreed on common rules on jurisdiction and enforcement of judgments in civil and commercial matters now known as the Brussels I Regulation, but this always excluded succession issues. In 1993, the Maastricht Treaty identified judicial co-operation in civil matters as an area of common interest for EU Member States. The Treaty of Amsterdam made judicial co-operation in civil matters a European Community policy linked to the free circulation of people.

The Lisbon Treaty came into force on December 1, 2009 and set out the current basis for European Union law making. A working knowledge of the structure of the consolidated versions of the EU Treaties is helpful when trying to understand the European Union law making process. The Rome Treaty Establishing the European Community and the Maastricht Treaty on the European Union, have been replaced by the Treaty on the European Union ("TEU") and the Treaty on the Functioning of the European Union ("TFEU").

Title V of Part Three of TFEU deals with what is now known as the Area of Freedom, Security and Justice. Chapter 3 of Title V of Part Three of TFEU deals with judicial co-operation in civil matters, including succession and the Regulation. It is under this chapter that succession matters have been addressed.

What was the problem?

Different EU Member States had completely different private international law rules for succession. For example, some used "domicile" but with a different definition from the common law one. The private international law of the majority of EU member states previously ruled that succession law was governed by the law of an individual's nationality and that the entire estate both movable and immovable was governed by that law. Whether "law" meant that state's internal law or included its private international law, i.e. whether renvoi was accepted, and whether directly forwards or backwards or also indirectly, varied from state to state. Renvoi is complex and is looked at in detail in Chapter 22.

There was no agreement between legal systems as to which was the applicable law. A court decision or inheritance certificate in one member state was not recognised, accepted or enforced in another. The conflicts involved were often irreconcilable and certainly added expense and time in the administration of estates with cross border elements.

There are terminology problems around the world and particularly across the Atlantic. Private international law as known in Europe is usually known as conflicts rules or conflicts of laws in the Americas. Applicable Law is often known in the Americas as the choice of law. In the EU, "choice of law" is often used for a professio juris or the ability for an individual to make a choice as to the succession law that is to apply. These issues are considered in chapter 2.

The European Union and the Single Market

The harmonisation of private international law for succession was first declared a priority in 1998. The Dörner and Lagarde Report was published in 2002 and the Commission Green Paper on Wills and Succession in 2005. The draft of a Succession Regulation was then published in October 2009.

The Regulation had to be agreed by both the EU Parliament and the Council of Ministers and was subject to qualified majority voting (under the old rules, the new Lisbon qualified majority voting rules not coming into effect until 2014).

The most detailed analysis and critique of the draft Succession Regulation was probably provided by the Max Planck Institute of Hamburg published in Rabels Zeitschrift 74 (2010) issue 3 but available via the EU Parliament website.[1]

The Max Planck Institute proposals did not suggest any changes in relation to the definition of habitual residence but did suggest some limits

---

1 https://www.europarl.europa.eu/document/activities/cont/201005/20100526ATT75035/20100526ATT75035EN.pdf

to clawback and various other additional suggestions including:

- choice of jurisdiction
- further elements as to choice of applicable law
- provisions for harmonisation as to formal validity of Wills

The Report is a useful summary of many issues and repays study.

Negotiations at the Council of Ministers level were confidential to a degree. An interim document was published on 6 June 2011.[2] A final version (18475/11 ADD 1 JUSTCIV 356 CODEC 2397 - "JUSTCIV 356")[3] was published on 15 December 2011, subject to further discussions and agreement on the issues of administration and clawback.

Political agreement was finally reached in March 2012 and the final Succession Regulation (EU) No.650/2012 entered into force on 17 August 2012. However, most of the Regulation did not apply until 17 August 2015.

Opt ins

Although approval of the Regulation was subject to qualified majority voting, Ireland (and the UK whilst it was a Member State) has an individual continuing opt-in choice in relation to matters within Title V Area of Freedom, Security and Justice under Protocol 21 annexed to TEU and to TFEU. Title V Regulations did not apply to Ireland (or to the UK) unless within three months of the proposal being made, Ireland (or the UK) decided to opt in under Article 3 of Protocol 21. Under the

2 http://register.consilium.europa.eu/pdf/en/11/st11/st11067.en11.pdf

3 http://register.consilium.europa.eu/pdf/en/11/st18/st18475.-ad01.en11.pdf

Irish constitution, such decision has to be ratified by the Irish Parliament.

The UK and Ireland separately decided not to opt in to the Regulation. The UK and Ireland took full part in the negotiations on the detail of the Regulation, but not having opted in, could not take part in the qualified majority voting. However, Ireland can, under Article 4 of Protocol 21, still opt in at a later stage, if it wishes.

Denmark is also not bound by Title V matters by virtue of Protocol 22. However, Denmark has no ability to opt in, unless it agrees to the revocation of Protocol 22 and to be bound by all Title V matters as a whole. In 2015, by referendum Denmark decided to retain its Protocol 22 opt out.

No other Member State has any such opt-in rights, and the Regulation, in the same manner as other EU regulations (other than those under enhanced co-operation), but unlike EU Directives, apply directly without any further local legislation. The Regulation once fully effective therefore automatically became the binding law within the 25 Member States and overrode conflicting provisions in local member state civil codes or legislation.

Notwithstanding the fact that Denmark and Ireland (and the UK whilst it was a Member State) are not bound by or affected by the Regulation, it is still part of the overall EU legislation or Acquis and may therefore be the subject of overriding treaty obligations between all Member States and its operation within the 25 Member States bound by it acknowledged by these other two non-participating Member States.

Following the 2016 Referendum in the UK, notice was served by it in March 2017 under Article 50 TEU with a view to the UK leaving the EU by April 2019, subsequently extended by agreement to 31 January 2020. Under the Withdrawal Agreement, the UK continued to be treated within the EU as if it were still a Member State until 31 December 2020. However, since the UK has never been bound by the Regulation, the fact that the UK is no longer an EU Member State generally, will not have any direct effect on the working of the Regulation, other than to clarify for the purposes of art.34 and renvoi that it definitely is not a Member State (see chapter 22).

Nevertheless, from the perspective of a third State, the Regulation still applies to assets situated in the 25 Member States that are participating, to which the Regulation applies (all EU Member States other than Denmark and Ireland – "the SR Zone"), to the succession of persons dying habitually resident there or to nationals of such states who make a valid *professio juris*, a valid choice of such states' law. It is important to understand that the Regulation governs the private international law for succession in the SR Zone, not only between participating Member States but also between both participating Member States and the non-participating member states, Denmark and Ireland, and also between participating Member States and third States outside the EU.

The Regulation may also apply when the private international law of Denmark or Ireland or of a third State directs the applicable law to be one within the SR Zone and does not accept any renvoi. The provisions of the Regulation are thus very important for all practitioners outside as well as inside the SR Zone to understand in any event.

The Need for Regulation

The Commission in the European Judicial Network website in 2012 stated that the Succession Regulation "should considerably simplify the rules on successions with an international dimension in the European Union. The aim is to make life easier for citizens by laying down common rules enabling the competent authority and law applicable to the body of assets making up a succession, wherever they may be, to be easily identified. In addition to providing more effective guarantees for the rights of heirs, legatees and other interested parties, the proposed Regulation will take some of the stress out of succession planning by enabling people to choose the law that will govern the transmission of all their assets. The European Commission is also proposing the creation of a European Certificate of Succession enabling heirs or the administrators of a succession to prove their capacity easily throughout the EU." There is much debate as to whether the Regulation has considerably simplified the rules in all cases. Probably, for many simpler cases, it has.

Legal Basis

One of the arcane issues of any EU legislation is its legal basis. All EU legislation must be based on an article of the TFEU. Thus, article 81 TFEU deals with 'judicial co-operation in civil matters having cross border implications, based on the principle of mutual recognition of judgments.' Article 81(2) sets out some of the general aims, but article 81(3) makes it clear that any such matters relating to family law must be passed unanimously (under special legislative procedure) rather than by majority voting. Article 114, by contrast, deals with the 'approximation of laws'. The precise legal basis for EU legislation has sometimes become a political football. Under protocol 21, the Ireland has (and the UK had) an opt-in arrangement for any Title V, Part III TFEU measures. Therefore, whether or not a measure is based on an article within that Part affects the right of Ireland to decide whether to opt-in or not.

The Regulation on Public Documents (EU) 2016/1191 was based on article 114 TFEU rather than article 81 TFEU; it did not give the UK any rights not to opt-in under protocol 21. The UK sometimes unsuccessfully attempted to argue that protocol 21 should apply whenever legislation touched upon Title V Part III matters, even if not so based.

The EU Parliament produced a helpful working document on this issue in December 2015. It reminded that the Court of Justice of the European Union (CJEU) guidance states that civil procedure should be dealt with under article 81 TFEU, while article 114 TFEU should deal with the internal market.

The relevance of this is that the mechanisms by which legislation is produced has a direct bearing on its shape. Whether legislation requires all member states or only a majority of states to agree, creates a very different political landscape. Whether a single member state has a veto or not, can produce very different results.

The Commission's Explanatory Report[4] referred to this issue in some detail at para.3.1:

> "Article 67(5) of the Treaty stipulates that the Council may take the measures provided for in Article 65 using the co-decision procedure laid down in Article 251 of the Treaty, except with regard to "aspects relating to family law".

It should first be emphasized that the vast majority of Member States, with the exception of the Nordic countries, classify the law of succession as a matter distinct from family law on account of the fact that it mainly covers property. Even at the level of substantive law, there are significant differences between the two matters. The main aim of the law of succession is to define the rules for passing on the inheritance and for regulating the transfer of the inheritance itself. Unlike inheritance law, the objective of family law is to govern above all the legal relationships linked to marriage and partnerships, filiation and the civil status of persons. Its basic social function is to protect family ties. Moreover, in contrast to family law, where the wishes of individuals play a very minor role and the vast majority of ties are governed by public policy, the law of succession remains a matter where the wishes of the entitled party play an important role.

There is therefore sufficient autonomy within these two branches of civil law for these matters to be treated separately from each other. Furthermore, as this is an exception, Article 67(5), second indent, of the Treaty must continue to be interpreted and applied strictly by the

---

4 COM (2009) 154 Final of 14 October 2009 https://www.europarl.europa.eu/meetdocs/2009_2014/documents/com/com_com%282009%290154_/com_com%282009%290154_en.pdf

institutions. The exception is therefore not applicable to this Regulation as far as succession is concerned."

Sweden, as one of the Nordic countries, attempted to argue, but failed in its attempt, that the Regulation was a matter of family law requiring unanimity. It did not require unanimity, and passed on the basis of majority voting.

In the UK all matters relating to divorce tend to be lumped together. A court will take jurisdiction and apply its own law to matters of divorce, parental responsibility, matrimonial property and maintenance obligations. UK family practitioners as a result very rarely, if ever, consider matters of foreign law.

Succession issues, by contrast, in the UK are divided between matters of formal and substantive validity of testamentary dispositions, administration of estates and the material applicable succession law. UK private client practitioners are therefore very used to applying different laws to various aspects of a succession.

Because of the differences under articles 81(2) and (3) TFEU, we have seen a salami slicing approach which deals with separate slices of the issues under separate regulations affecting private international law and divorce (in the broadest sense) but a contrasting kitchen sink approach or everything thrown in together for succession.

In relation to divorce we have seen the Brussels II Regulation (EC) No 2201/2003 (Brussels II bis) that deals with jurisdiction, recognition and enforcement for divorce and parental responsibility and Rome III as the enhanced co-operation measure (since it was not possible to obtain unanimity for a regulation) dealing with applicable law on divorce. The Maintenance Obligations Regulation (EC) No 4/2009 deals with jurisdiction, recognition and enforcement for maintenance obligations and the 2007 Hague Protocol deals with applicable law of maintenance obligations. The Enhanced co-operation Regulations on Matrimonial Property Regimes (EU) No 2016/1103 and on the Property Effects of

Registered Partnerships (EU) No 2016/1104 have been effective with transitional provisions in 18 member states since January 2019 and are referred to in chapter 13. Rome III, another enhanced co-operation Regulation, does not apply in Croatia, Cyprus, Czech Republic, Denmark, Estonia, Finland, Ireland, Netherlands, Poland, Slovakia, Sweden (and never applied in the UK). The 2007 Hague Protocol does apply in all EU member states including Ireland, but not in Denmark and the UK. It is the legislative straitjacket that compels the EU Commission to obtain unanimity among member states in relation to family-law matters that has produced this very confusing mess.[5]

It was inevitable when the EU Commission turned to matters of succession and in legislating outside the confines of article 82(3) that it was bound to go overboard and throw in the kitchen sink. The Regulation was the most ambitious (and some would argue, imperialistic) piece of EU legislation to date. Not only does it include issues of jurisdiction; recognition and enforcement and applicable law, often on a worldwide basis, in relation to every conceivable aspect of succession including administration; but also formal and substantive validity not just of testamentary dispositions, but also succession agreements. It also includes the new European Certificate of Succession and the acceptance and enforcement of notarial and other instruments.

It is important to remember that the Regulation applies to matters that in the UK and other third States may not be classified as succession. Succession under the Regulation includes not only inheritance but also administration and the validity of written dispositions of property upon death. The particular complexities of clawback and the uncertainties and extent to which it is actually a matter within succession is considered in chapter 18.

In third States, the different connecting factors of the different areas

[5] Not helped in the UK by the application of the Maintenance Obligations Regulation internally, but not Brussels II *bis*, *Villiers v Villiers* [2020] UKSC 30

within the Regulation's definition of succession must be kept firmly in mind.

It is perhaps the over-ambitious scope of the Regulation that brings with it so much complexity and uncertainty. If it had been less ambitious, it is more likely that the UK and Ireland might have opted in.

Language and Constructive Ambiguity

The difficulties of agreeing EU wide legislation across differing legal systems and in 24 languages is formidable. Draft Regulations are often first prepared in French and then subsequently translated. Differing threads of translation can produce subtle changes and yet each language version is to have equal weight.

Constructive ambiguity as a term and the uncertainties that it brings are much discredited. However, each piece of European Union legislation is a pragmatic compromise. In order for a regulation to be agreed and to work, an element of uncertainty is inevitable if it is to be broad enough to apply across all of the EU different legal systems and languages. Such ambiguities are only resolved as and when they reach the CJEU. However, many of the particular ambiguities within the Regulation are still appearing out of the woodwork.

Comitology

Comitology is a form of delegated legislation similar to a Statutory Instrument in the UK. A Regulation can give the Commission implementing powers and can also stipulate that the Commission is to be assisted by a committee when drafting the resulting implementing regulation. Some implementing regulations, if uncontroversial, can be adopted by the Commission, otherwise, they must be approved by a qualified majority.

The Court of Justice of the European Union (CJEU)

The CJEU is divided into two courts, the Court of Justice that deals with requests for preliminary rulings from national courts, certain actions for annulment and appeals and the General Court that rules on actions for annulment brought by individuals, companies and, in some cases, EU governments. In practice, this means that the General Court deals mainly with competition law, State aid and the like. The judges and advocates general are appointed jointly by national governments. In each Court, the judges select their President.

In the Court of Justice, each case is assigned a judge-rapporteur, and one advocate general. In the General Court the procedure is similar, save that most cases are heard by three judges and there are no advocates general. Cases in both courts usually proceed with an initial written stage and then an oral stage.

The parties give written statements to the Court. Observations can also be submitted by national authorities, EU institutions and sometimes private individuals. All of this is summarised by the judge-rapporteur and then discussed at the Court's general meeting, which decides whether a public hearing needs to be held, whether an official opinion from the advocate general is necessary, and how many judges will deal with the case, depending on the importance and complexity of the case.

At the public hearing, lawyers from both sides put their case to and are questioned by the judges and the advocate general. If the Court has decided an Opinion of the advocate general is necessary, this is given some weeks after the hearing. The judges then deliberate and give their verdict.

CJEU decisions coming from a civil law tradition are unanimous and are therefore always concise. There is no scope for dissenting opinions or obiter dicta. This can puzzle and annoy common law practitioners. However, what is not stated is often as important as what is.

CURIA[6] is the home website for the CJEU where further details of the courts, copies of judgments and advocate general opinions and details of forthcoming cases can be found.

Other Institutions

The Hague Conference (HccH)

The Hague Conference on Private International Law (HccH) is an intergovernmental organisation currently with 84 individual state members. The European Union is also a member as a Regional Economic Integration Organisation.

The statutory mission of HccH is to work for the progressive unification of PIL rules. It attempts to find internationally agreed approaches to the PIL concepts of jurisdiction, applicable law, and the recognition and enforcement of judgments in areas ranging from commercial law, banking law and international civil procedure, to child protection, marriage and personal status. It generally meets every four years in plenary session to negotiate and adopt conventions and to decide upon future work. The conventions are prepared by special commissions or working groups held several times a year, usually at The Hague. The HccH working language was originally only French, but since 1960 has been both English and French.

The most widely ratified conventions deal with a broad range of topics: the abolition of legalisation – Apostille [HccH 12], service of proceedings [HccH 14], the taking of evidence abroad [HccH 20], access to justice [HccH 29], international child abduction [HccH28], cross border adoption [HccH 33], formal validity of wills and testaments [HccH 11], maintenance obligations [HccH 23, HccH 24 and HccH 39] and recognition of divorce [HccH 18].

---

6 https://curia.europa.eu/jcms/jcms/j_6/en/

In addition to HccH 11, the Conventions that are of particular relevance to the Regulation are:

- The Convention of 5 October 1961 Abolishing the Requirement of Legalisation for Foreign Public Documents[7] ('HccH 12') ratified by all EU Member States, other than Bulgaria, Italy, Latvia, Lithuania, Portugal and Romania;

- The Convention of 2 October 1973 Concerning the International Administration of the Estates of Deceased Persons[8] ('HccH 21') ratified by Czechia, Portugal and Slovakia;

- The Convention of 1 August 1989 on the Law Applicable to Succession to the Estates of Deceased Persons[9] ('HccH 32') that had been ratified by the Netherlands but because of the implementation of the Regulation, HccH 32 was denounced by the Netherlands with effect from 1 April 2015;

- The Convention of 19 October 1996 on Jurisdiction, Applicable Law, Recognition, Enforcement and Co-operation in Respect of Parental Responsibility and Measures for the Protection of Children[10] ('HccH 34') ratified by all EU Member States and also Norway, Switzerland and the UK.

Ratification creates the legal obligation for the ratifying state to apply the convention. The HccH website, www.hcch.net, is a very useful resource that sets out updated information on the Hague Conventions, the texts of the various Conventions, status reports as to those States that have signed, ratified or acceded, bibliographies, information regarding the

---

7 https://www.hcch.net/en/instruments/conventions/full-text/?cid=41

8 https://www.hcch.net/en/instruments/conventions/full-text/?cid=83

9 https://www.hcch.net/en/instruments/conventions/full-text/?cid=62

10 https://www.hcch.net/en/instruments/conventions/full-text/?cid=70

central authorities and explanatory reports.

ICC/CIEC

The International Commission on Civil Status (ICCS)/(CIEC) Commission Internationale de l'Etat Civil[11] is an intergovernmental organisation whose aim is to facilitate international co-operation in civil status matters and to improve the operation of national civil status departments. To this end, it keeps up to date documentation on legislation and case law setting out the law of the member States, provides those States with information and expertise, carries out legal and technical studies, prepares publications and drafts Conventions and Recommendations.

Whilst the United Kingdom was a member it did not ratify any of the ICCS conventions. The guide to civil status in the UK is however of value.[12] ICCS has however become less significant since it has now lost most of its European Members. Its current members are now only Belgium, Luxembourg, Spain, Switzerland and Turkey.

---

11 http://www.ciec1.org

12 http://www.ciec1.org/SITECIEC/PAGE_GP_Pays/

CHAPTER TWO

PRIVATE INTERNATIONAL LAW

Introduction

'Private international law is that part of law which comes into play when the issue before the court is so closely connected with a foreign system of law as to necessitate recourse to that system'[13]

Private international law (PIL) deals primarily with the application of laws in space and time to decide the circumstances in which foreign law will apply. The local courts at a particular time are sovereign and can define as they wish, and place a boundary at that or any other time as they think appropriate. Unlike garden fences, the boundaries created by separate countries' legal systems rarely meet, and can be in different places at different times. Each country has its own separate and distinct Private International Law rules which do not necessarily mesh with the PIL of another state.

Federal states, such as Australia, Canada, the United Kingdom and the United States of America, are themselves subdivided into numbers of separate individual areas with different legal systems. Such individual legal areas are often known as 'law districts'.

Nomenclature causes its own difficulties. In common law states, the subject may be known as Conflict of Laws or Conflicts of Laws whilst it is known as Private International Law (PIL) or International Private Law in civil law states.

[13] Private International Law – Cheshire, North and Fawcett 14th Edition.

It is common in all different private international law rules, to consider separately, issues of:

- Jurisdiction – do the courts of a state consider that they have jurisdiction to deal with a matter in the first place?

- Applicable Law or Choice of Law – if they do, which state's laws will be applied?

- Recognition and Enforcement – if the courts of a state make a particular order, will that order be recognised in and enforce by the courts of a different state?

- Acceptance and enforcement or admissibility and circulation of documents

In Europe "choice of law" usually means the ability to make a choice; a *professio juris.*

'International Private Law' may sometimes be a wider term than that of Private International Law and can include comparative law issues.

'Conflict of Law' is sometimes used differently, as a term to mean solely the Applicable Law issues of PIL.

'Choice of law' can be used to mean either the Applicable Law or also as a *professio juris* or the ability of a party to make their own particular valid choice as to the law that will be applicable.[14]

In this book, the term Private International Law (PIL) is used broadly to include matters of jurisdiction, applicable law, recognition of court orders

---

14 Katharina Boele-Woelki's book "Unifying and Harmonizing Substantive Laws and the Role of Conflict of Laws" Hague Pocketbook is very helpful on these matters.

and acceptance of documents and their enforcement.

Jurisdiction can mean the legal competence of a court to consider a particular issue. It can also mean the extent of a particular law district. To avoid confusion, the term is used to mean legal competence.

Recognition generally relates to the effectiveness of an order of a foreign court. Since succession will require grants of representation that may not necessarily be issued by a court, and may include agreements made directly between beneficiaries, that are not court orders and therefore are not capable of recognition, PIL must include the acceptance and enforcement of such documents in other law districts.

PIL has been heavily influenced by the leading works on the subject. Dicey[15] and Cheshire in England and Wales, Anton in Scotland,[16] Beale in the USA,[17] Savigny,[18] Story,[19] and many others. It has developed academically over the years and numbers of different theories discussed. Theories of acquired rights or of local law were replaced by theories of law selection or jurisdiction selection.

Reference is often made to the 'comity of nations', but modern authors are sceptical that the term has any real meaning or justification. Applying a law other than that of the jurisdiction is not for the purposes of courtesy but in order to achieve the most appropriate result.

---

15 Lord Collins of Mapesbury et al, eds., *Dicey, Morris & Collins on the Conflicts of Law*, 16th ed. (London: Sweet & Maxwell, 2022)

16 Paul Beaumont and Peter McEleavy, *Anton's Private International Law* (3rd Edition, Sweet & Maxwell, 2012)

17 Joseph H Beale (1861 – 1943), *A Treatise on the Conflict of Laws* (Baker, Voorhis & Co, 1935)

18 Friedrich Carl von Savigny (1779 - 1861), *System des heutigens Römischen Rechts* (Berlin 1849)

19 Joseph Story (1779 – 1845), *Commentaries on the Conflicts of Laws* (Boston 1834)

Private International Law Concepts

Characterisation / Classification / Qualification

Characterisation or classification was invented as a means of legal analysis at the end of the nineteenth century, but not introduced to the law of England and Wales as a concept until the 1930's. The topic is known as *qualification* in French and as *qualifikation* in German law. Once a court has satisfied itself that it has jurisdiction, it must then decide the nature of the legal issue before it. Different categories or classes of topics of law will have different connecting factors. A matter of contract may be governed in the European Union by the Rome I Regulation. Jurisdiction and recognition in a matter of divorce or parental responsibility may be governed by the Brussels II *bis* Regulation.

The more difficult question is as to which rules of classification of which State should be applied. The choice is usually between using the rules of classification of the law of the forum, or the rules of the state whose law is to be applied, although this can produce circular arguments. In England & Wales, in practice, the law of the forum, i.e. English rules of classification are generally used. The rules of classification themselves, are always influenced by the international law issues involved.

Where matters of PIL are to be considered, local law distinctions may give way to more widely recognised ones. Thus, the common law distinction between real and personal property gives way in PIL matters to the distinction between that of immovable and movable property. Whilst some law districts may decide that whether property should be classified as movable or immovable property is a matter for the law of the forum, PIL in England and Wales generally holds that this is a question to be decided according to the law of the place where the property is situated.

The direct private international law issues linked to succession and that are the topics for this book are:

- Which court or authority has jurisdiction to make orders or certificates, whether in non-contentious probate matters or in contentious disputes, in relation to an estate and the assets of the deceased? Where will a succession be opened and a certificate of inheritance issued?

- Which state's law will that court or authority apply and will it apply different laws to movables and to immovables?

- Will a law district recognise and enforce an order of the courts of another law district and if so, will it apply local conditions of implementation?

- Will a law district accept and enforce a form of inheritance certificate from an authority or an agreement between beneficiaries, if it is valid in another law district?

The terminology that is used in PIL in this context is not altogether straightforward, because the terms used in the Regulation are not necessarily those that would be used in individual jurisdictions. For example, the definitions in art.3 of "succession", "agreement as to succession", "joint will", "disposition of property upon death" (DoPuD), and "court" are (still to the surprise of some member states) autonomous. Similarly, for a common law practitioner, terms such as the "opening of the succession" or "heir" are not familiar.

Incidental Questions

Many legal issues involve more than one question. The jurisdiction, applicable law and recognition issues for the main question will be governed by the PIL of the relevant state. Incidental questions such as whether property is movable or immovable, or the validity of marriage or the admissibility of a Will, may be governed by the same law as the main question or may be classified as a separate legal question and dealt with under its own separate PIL.

Connecting Factors

Different categories or classes of topics of law will have different connecting factors to establish jurisdiction, applicable law and recognition and enforcement. The connecting factors may be a concept such as the domicile, nationality or habitual residence of a party, a law chosen by a party ('*professio juris*') or the situation or the *situs* of property.

Most states which can trace their civil code to influences from the German BGB, have historically regarded questions of inheritance (whether movable or immovable) as a matter for the 'personal law' of the individual usually governed by the law of the nationality.

By contrast common law states and states which can trace their civil code to influences from the French Napoleonic code, have historically regarded questions of inheritance of movables as a matter for the 'personal law' of the individual usually governed by the law of the deceased's domicile whilst immovables are subject to the law of the *situs*.

Lord Hope of Craighead in *Mark v Mark*[20] set out the distinction between personal law or civil status and public law or political status:

> "The answer to this question is, I think, to be found in the distinction to which Lord Westbury drew attention at the start of his speech in *Udny v Udny* (1869) LR 1 Sc & Div 441, 457:
>
> > 'The law of England, and of almost all civilized countries, ascribes to each individual at his birth two distinct legal states or conditions; one by virtue of which he becomes the subject of some particular country, binding him by the tie of natural allegiance, and which may be called his political *status*; another, by virtue of which he has ascribed to him the character of a citizen of some particular country, and as such is possessed of certain municipal rights, and subject to certain obligations,

[20] [2006] 1 AC 98 at paragraphs 4 and 5.

> which latter character is the civil *status* or condition of the individual, and may be quite different from his political status. The political *status* may depend on different laws in different countries; whereas the civil *status* is governed universally by one single principle, namely, that of domicil, which is the criterion established by law for the purpose of determining civil *status*. For it is on this basis that the personal rights of the party, that is to say, the law which determines his majority or minority, his marriage, succession, testacy, or intestacy, must depend.'

Translated into language with which we are familiar today, the point that Lord Westbury was making was that cases where a question of public law is in issue must be distinguished from cases where the issue is one of private law. Public law issues raise questions which concern what Lord Westbury described as the person's political status. The criteria by which status for the purpose of these questions is to be judged may differ from country to country, according to the rules that it lays down as to who may lawfully enter or lawfully remain there. Private law issues, on the other hand, are referred to the law of the person's domicile. The criteria for the determination of a person's domicile are governed by a single principle which ought to be capable of being applied universally. The importance of this distinction has not always been recognised."

The precise meaning and definition for each connecting factor will vary between law districts. Domicile in one state will not be defined in the same way in a different state.

The connecting factors of domicile and nationality will still often be relevant, notwithstanding the fact that the Regulation mainly uses the connecting factor of habitual residence. There will be many matters and incidental questions outside the scope of the Regulation, still governed by the law of the traditional connecting factor. Many preliminary questions such as the status of a particular relationship and other matters excluded by art.1, will be governed by the law of the traditional connecting factor.

It should be remembered that the connecting factor in UK PIL for the administration of an estate is generally *situs*. Different aspects of the Regulation will be governed by differing connecting factors outside the EU.

Domicile

Domicile is used as the traditional civil status connecting factor in England and Wales, Scotland, Northern Ireland, Ireland, many Commonwealth countries and the United States of America. The precise definition of domicile can be different in each law district.

The Law Commission of England and Wales reviewed the concept of domicile in 1987 and its report is a useful analysis.[21] The Law Reform Commission of Hong Kong Report on Rules for Determining Domicile of April 2005[22] is another excellent summary of the law of domicile in differing law districts.

The general position is that a child takes a domicile of origin from its parents, will have a domicile of dependency until it is able to establish its own independent domicile and can then establish a domicile of choice. The manner in which the rules work are arcane and vary considerably from one law district to another.

In Scotland[23] a child takes its domicile of origin from its parents or if their domiciles differ, from the jurisdiction with which it has the closest connection. In the remainder of the United Kingdom a legitimate child takes its domicile of origin from its father, an illegitimate child from its mother. There are specific rules in relation to adopted and orphaned

21 Law Commission, Private International Law: Law of Domicile, (Law Com No 168, 1987).

22 Available at http://www.hkreform.gov.hk/en/publications/rdomicile.htm, accessed 14 May 2014.

23 By the Family Law (Scotland) Act 2006

children.[24]

Women on marriage often assumed a domicile of dependency on their husbands. This rule was changed in England and Wales in 1974[25] and declared unconstitutional in Ireland in 1992[26] with retroactive effect from 1938. The rule however continues in India.

Thereafter on reaching a specified age,[27] an individual can acquire a domicile of choice. This may be acquired by both actually residing in a law district and having an intention to make one's home in that place, permanently or indefinitely, amounting to a fixed and settled purpose, a determination or a final and deliberate intention to abandon the country of former domicile and to settle in the new country of residence.[28]

In the United Kingdom, if a person abandons a domicile of choice without immediately acquiring another domicile of choice, the domicile of origin automatically revives irrespective of intention. Other common law districts, such as India, Australia, New Zealand and the United States of America, have developed the rule that the old domicile of choice continues.

For persons who do not have sufficient mental capacity to establish an independent domicile of choice, the rules can vary. In Scotland, domicile is the domicile that a person had on reaching the age of 16 or at the onset of incapacity whichever is the later. In the remainder of the United Kingdom, if the incapacity *predates* 16, domicile continues to be determined as if he were an unmarried person under 16, i.e. a domicile of dependency subject to changes of domicile of the parent on which they

24 Domicile & Matrimonial Proceedings Act 1973

25 By the Domicile & Matrimonial Proceedings Act 1973

26 In the case of *W v W* [1993] 2IR 476

27 Now 16 throughout the United Kingdom, but a different age may apply elsewhere.

28 *IRC v Bullock* [1976] 1WLR 1178 (Court of Appeal)

are dependent. If the incapacity *postdates* 16, domicile is that as at the onset of incapacity.

Nationality

In the nineteenth century, as nation states emerged, nationality often replaced domicile as the connecting factor in most countries of Europe such as Austria, Germany, Greece, Italy, Portugal and Spain. Its use spread to South America and Japan.

The use of nationality as a connecting factor does sometimes produce problems with stateless persons such as asylum seekers and with persons from states that have varying political recognition such as Northern Cyprus, Taiwan, Kosovo or Palestine.

For persons with dual nationality, there is no concept of a primary nationality and generally, jurisdictions tend to apply their own law or the law of nationality with which the person is most closely connected. This can therefore produce conflicting results. Similarly there are problems with Federal and composite States that include different separate law districts with differing laws, whether differentiated by area or an individual factor such as religion. Often the internal rules of such federal states are used to determine the law district with which the citizen is most closely connected.

Habitual Residence

Habitual residence in the context of the Regulation is considered in Chapter 4.

Situs

The place where an asset is situated can often be a relevant connecting factor. Courts will often regard themselves as having jurisdiction in relation to assets situated within their geographical law district. It should be remembered that *situs* is generally the connecting factor in UK PIL for the law governing the administration of an estate.

At first glance, the identity of the place where an asset is situated should be easy to establish. However, there can be numbers of complications.

Registered Securities

Registered securities are often regarded as being situated in the country holding the register of title, or if duplicates are held in more than one country, the country where in the ordinary course of business, the transfer could most conveniently be effected. Some states however, may regard them as being situated in the state in which the business has its seat.

Bare Trusts and Nominee Arrangements and Mandates

Often the underlying interest is deemed to be situated where the underlying property that is held is actually situated. This is often surprising to many. The Convention of 5 July 2006 on the Law Applicable to Certain Rights in Respect of Securities held with an Intermediary ('HccH 36'), provides rules in relation to securities held by nominees and uses the Place of Relevant Intermediary Approach ('PRIMA') in force since April 1, 2017, having been ratified by Switzerland, Mauritius and the United States of America.

Debts and choses in action

Debts, contract debts and choses in action are usually situated in the country of the debtor or where payment or the contract can be enforced. A company debt will usually be situated in the country of the head office unless the contract locates it at a particular branch. A bank debt will often be deemed situated in the country of the branch holding the account. However, some states may look to the state of the nationality of the named account holder.

Cryptocurrency and other Digital Assets

The Property (Digital Assets) Bill 2024 if passed would define digital assets as personal property rights within England & Wales and Northern Ireland.

Tangible Movables and Chattels

Movables and chattels are generally regarded as being situated where they are actually located. A ship or aircraft is often deemed to be where it is located, if it is within territorial waters or airspace, otherwise where it may be deemed to be in the place where it is registered.

Immovable Property

Immovable property is usually situated where it is located. This also usually includes property, owned, but subject to a binding contract for sale and also a purchaser's interest in a binding contract to buy, although subject to the obligation to pay the purchase price or an option to purchase immovable property.

Business, Partnerships and Goodwill

An interest in a partnership is generally movable, not immovable property (even if the partnership owns immovable property) and is situated where, the principal place of business, is located. Goodwill is usually inseparable from the business. However, in some jurisdictions a partnership has legal personality and may be regarded as a corporate structure.

Interests in the Estate of a deceased Person in the course of Administration

Property still held by Personal Representatives who are administering the estate of a deceased person, is often deemed to be situated in the place where the Personal Representatives can be compelled to administer the estate. If there are no Personal Representatives, then the property may be deemed to be situated in the place of principal administration, which may be the place of domicile of the deceased. This too can produce unexpected results and differences.

Interests in Trusts

If the concept of a trust is recognised then the place of an interest in a trust is often dependent on whether or not there is a beneficial interest in the trust.

If there is no beneficial interest in the trust (which might include a reversionary interest), it is situated where action may be brought against the trustees, usually the place of the residence of the trustees.

If there is a beneficial interest in the trust, it is usually deemed to be situated where the trust property is located.

Choice of Law – *Professio Juris*

The ability of a party to choose which state is to have jurisdiction or as to the law that is to be applicable varies considerably. Party autonomy is often favoured in matters of contract law or the law applicable to a trust, but less so in relation to other legal classes.

Jurisdiction

In England and Wales, jurisdiction in actions *in personam* has been based on the presence of the defendant in the country, the defendant submitting to the jurisdiction of the court or a statutory right to serve the defendant outside the country. Actions *in rem* were based on the presence of the thing within the country. In relation to some legal classes, the parties may have autonomy and can select in a choice of court or jurisdiction agreement, the forum that is to have jurisdiction to deal with any disputes between them.

In matters of probate, the earlier cases show that the jurisdiction of the courts of England and Wales was based on the physical presence of an executor or administrator in England and Wales. If an administrator was not present in England and Wales, the court had no jurisdiction, but could order the appointment of one.

The courts have jurisdiction over the administrator and the estate situated in England and Wales, whatever the residence, domicile or nationality of the deceased.

In other states, jurisdiction may be based on the *situs* of property in that state or upon the last residence or nationality of the deceased in the state.

Competing Jurisdictions

If there are numbers of different possible jurisdictions, then questions will arise as to which one is the most appropriate. Under some EU Regulations, there can be a race to the forum, on the basis that the first claim validly issued, will fix the relevant jurisdiction.

In other circumstances, parallel proceedings or *lis alibi pendens* or *lis pendens* can subsist. Means therefore often exist in order to limit competing proceedings.

In England and Wales, there has been discretion for the court to permit a claim to be served outside the state on the grounds that it is the most appropriate forum or *forum conveniens.* The doctrine of refusing jurisdiction on the grounds of *forum non conveniens,* on the other hand, whilst existing in the USA and Scotland was not generally available in England and Wales until 1984.[29]

In some cases, the courts in England and Wales will grant an injunction

29 In the case of *The Abidin Daver* [1984] AC 795 and now set out in the leading case of *Spiliada Maritime Corp v Cansulex Ltd* [1987] AC 460.

in order to restrain foreign proceedings. (An anti-suit injunction. Other jurisdictions may order an anti-anti-suit injunction.[30] We have not yet had an anti-anti-anti-suit injunction.)

Some conventions and Regulations enable the transfer of jurisdiction from one state to another at the request of the courts of one of the states. Arts. 5 of the Regulation only accepts such a transfer in limited circumstances. These issues are considered further in chapter 9.

Applicable law

In many legal classes, the courts having jurisdiction in relation to a matter with foreign connections, will need to consider which law is to be applied. This is sometimes known as 'choice of law', but does not involve generally involve any party autonomy and will be subject to the particular PIL rules of the law district.

Foreign law theories – interests of the parties or interests of a foreign country

The reasons as to why the courts of a law district may apply a law other than its own, are usually divided by academics into the interests and expectations of the parties on the one hand and the interests of a foreign state on the other.

In some states, foreign law may be regarded as a matter of fact to be proved by one of the parties or expert evidence, whilst in other states, foreign law may be regarded as a matter of law, to be known by and established by the court. Proof of foreign law may therefore be dealt with in very different ways.

---

30 As in the case of 21 O 9512/19 Regional Court Munich I http://eplaw.org/wp-content/uploads/2019/12/DE-AASI-HRC-Munich-6-U-5042-19-EN.pdf

Substantive and Procedural Law

Whilst substantive law may be governed by a foreign law, matters of procedure are generally subject to the law of the forum. Whether a question is one of substance or of procedure is generally a matter for the forum. In common law states, the distinction can be regarded as one between rights and remedies. In other states, the distinction may appear artificial; rights and remedies are often inseparable. In practice, the distinction can be difficult to establish in practice and the fact that different law districts will classify matters as substantive when in another they may be regarded as procedural, often causes irresolvable conflicts.

Limitation of action was historically regarded as a procedural matter under the law of England and Wales, whilst in many civil law states, it will be regarded as substantive. Matters of evidence are usually regarded as procedural questions, but how evidence is interpreted may be an issue for the substantive law.

Renvoi

If the relevant connecting factor establishes that a foreign substantive law is to be applied, the question that has to be decided is whether or not the reference to the foreign law includes a reference to all of the PIL rules of that law or merely the internal foreign law with no reference to PIL.

Some jurisdictions will only apply the internal law, with no reference back or *renvoi*, whilst others may accept a reference back to its own law. Many systems distinguish between this remission, sending back or first degree *renvoi* (*Rückverweisung*) and transmission, sending on or second degree *renvoi* (*Weiterverweisung*).

Some states such as the United Kingdom, adopt the double or total *renvoi* or foreign court theory and apply the law that would be applied by the other court. The distinctions between remission and transmission are therefore not relevant for UK PIL.

It is desirable for the UK courts to reach the same decision as the foreign court for two principal reasons. First, where the foreign state has control over the subject matter of a dispute, the UK court must reach the same decision as the foreign court or else the judgement is likely to be unenforceable. This is perhaps clearest when considering disputes over title to immoveable property. Second, in certain circumstances it is critical for policy reasons for the UK court to reach the same decision as the foreign court. However, the doctrine of *renvoi* is not applied by the UK courts in all areas of law.

In general, the doctrine of renvoi is not applied to issues involving title to moveable property. In *Blue Sky One v Mahan Air*[31] the court reasoned that the doctrine was not suitable because it involved the English court preferring a foreign state's choice of law rules to its own, it was difficult to apply and it was unlikely to lead to greater uniformity of decision across jurisdictions.

However, the Hon. Mr Justice Eady in *Iran v Berend*[32] neatly summarised the English stance to the doctrine of *renvo*i in stating that although *renvoi* was not part of the choice of law rules in property, "the modern approach towards *renvoi* is that there is no over-arching doctrine to be applied, but it will be seen as a useful tool to be applied where appropriate".

For matters involving inheritance law, foreign law is generally applied and then this is usually the law that would be applied by the foreign court with *total renvoi.*

For matters involving administration courts and administrative authorities will usually be applying the local law.

The classic example of *renvoi* is that of *Re Annesley*[33] where, in accordance

31 [2010] EWHC 631

32 [2007] EWHC 132 QB

33 [1926] Ch 692

with the English test for domicile, a British subject died domiciled in France. The UK PIL rule provided for succession to her moveable property to be governed by French law as the law of the place of her domicile. However, under French law, the succession to her moveable property should be governed by the law of her nationality (ie English law, as most closely connected to her nationality). The English court held that a French court would apply the doctrine of *renvo*i and as such, apply the English PIL rules which provided for French law to govern the succession, which would then be accepted by the French court.

But the application of the doctrine is unpredictable. A court may only apply it if one party expressly pleads its use which adds to the expense and complexity of the litigation. Even then, the court has the safety net of public policy to invoke if the result of applying the doctrine offends concepts of justice or morality. *Renvoi* thus may be seen as another partially discretionary tool which enables justice to be achieved in the particular circumstances. This lack of certainty is one reason why *renvoi* is not seen as appropriate in commercial disputes. Further, the discretionary and flexible nature of the doctrine is contrary to the traditional concept that PIL rules should not be influenced by potential outcomes.

It should also be remembered that whilst achieving decisional harmony is an important objective of PIL, it is not an overriding objective. Having consistently incorrect decisions is not any better than inconsistent decisions. Renvoi has its detractors and is now often excluded.

It was to be excluded in the Regulation as initially drafted, but political pressures partially brought it back.

Recognition and Enforcement

In England and Wales, a foreign judgment could not be enforced directly, but did create an obligation that could itself be the subject of proceedings that could then be enforced.

Particular laws, treaties, conventions or Regulations may enable foreign judgments to be recognised and enforced. It is sometimes necessary to register the judgment or obtain a form of 'Exequatur' to enable it to be enforced. Recognition is only given to court judgments or judgments have effect as court judgments. Recognition cannot therefore be given to documents, private mandates or other documents that are not court judgments.

Public policy, penal/police laws, revenue laws, public laws

Notwithstanding that PIL may direct that a foreign judgment should be recognised and enforced, there may be local rules prohibiting the recognition or enforcement for specific reasons.

In civil law states, the doctrine of *ordre public* is designed to ensure that public welfare prevails. In common law states, matters of public policy such as fundamental rules of justice, human rights, morality or the interests of the state may override foreign law.

Historically, revenue laws were not directly or indirectly enforced across borders, although this principle is being eroded by many international agreements and conventions.

Penal, penalty or police laws involving enforcement of a foreign state's rights are generally not enforced.

These issues are further discussed in the next chapter.

CHAPTER THREE

SUCCESSION, IDENTITY AND CULTURE

Unlike contractual or non-contractual obligations, succession law varies very considerably indeed between Member States. The transfer of property on death, must collide with rules as to the transfer of property *inter vivos,* which generally is always subject to national substantive law. Some Member States classified the administration of an estate as separate from the applicable inheritance law and regarded it a matter of local procedure, whilst in others, the applicable succession law governed all aspects including the administration and inheritance. The inheritance rights of family members also vary considerably; from a light touch monetary claim in the Netherlands to rights *in rem* in Italy. Obligations to restore also vary from being limited to gratuitous transfers made two years prior to death in some Member States to full lifetime obligations in others. The detail of such obligations may also vary as to being valued as at the time of gift or at the time of death and may or may not exclude purchases of insurance contracts or acquisition of joint property with survivorship provisions. Such considerable variations and complications, mean that simple solutions to cross-border estates do not exist.

Mandatory family protection is not uniform across the EU. The concepts developed from Roman law through the *ius commune* into modern civil codes. The relevant rules of Roman law were simplified by the draftsmen of the 18th century codifications. Two models developed and were particularly influential. The 1811 Austrian Civil Code which Germany adopted defined a compulsory portion, i.e. a personal monetary claim. By contrast, the 1804 French Civil Code model of forced heirship reserved a part of the testator's property to closest relatives, and gave a right *in* rem. The French model was initially extremely influential, but many of the systems influenced by it have undergone subsequent changes.

Rights *in rem* have often been replaced by monetary claims. Mandatory family protection by means of a compulsory portion thus appears to have gained in popularity. The definition of relatives entitled to a compulsory portion also now tends to be drawn more narrowly than previously. In France, only descendants and not ascendants are generally now reserved heirs. The proportions given to reserved heirs have, also been lowered under many systems. There are also now more proposals to make mandatory family protection more flexible. The power to deprive a person of their right to a compulsory portion, or to become forced heir, has under some legal systems been extended and the concept of a needs-based claim for maintenance has been considered, or even implemented, particularly for the surviving spouse. The French *Cour de Cassation* has as discussed in chapter 24 linked public policy issues to the need for maintenance.

The other problem is cultural and psychological. Whilst it may be overstated to say that succession law is part of the cultural DNA of a legal system and its citizens, it is certainly true that the vast majority of lawyers, notaries and advisors only train in the detail of their local national system and shy away from foreign legal systems on which they have limited knowledge and may not be insured to advise. The culture of most states involves a history of obtaining independence, either from an Empire or a former monarchical system, and the civil codes and constitutions thus created incorporated succession law in their bedrock.

The principal reason for the creation of the EU was the desire to ensure that France and Germany never again went to war, and accordingly in the EU it is often regarded as bad manners and politically incorrect to refer to the detailed history of the 20th Century before 1945. Although, the silence on matters of recent history is understandable, it is not always helpful.

It was the 50th anniversary of the Molotov-Ribbentrop pact of 1939 that triggered the human chain of the Baltic Way in Estonia, Latvia and Lithuania that then led to the fall of the Iron Curtain. The Baltic States have only had truly independent modern existence between 1918 and 1940 and since 1991. Whilst Denmark, Ireland and the UK joined the EU in 1973, Greece in 1981, Portugal and Spain in 1986, Austria, Finland and Sweden in 1995, Cyprus, Czech Republic, Estonia, Hungary, Latvia, Lithuania, Malta, Poland, Slovakia, Slovenia all joined in 2004. Bulgaria and Romania joined in 2007 and Croatia in 2013. In 2015, Austria celebrated the 50th anniversary of its re-establishment in 1955.

In many of these states, the individual provisions of their succession law are part of the independent identity of the state. Many Member States that have had little independent existence until recently, are not keen to surrender items of national identity in favour of the EU after they may only recently have been wrested from Soviet control.

Issues of public policy are therefore impossible to separate from history and culture. Citizens and advisors, therefore, find it difficult to comprehend that the Regulation may affect the ways of succession to which they are accustomed and to the Regulation is brought from each Member State different preconceptions and interpretations. The breadth of the scope of the Regulation has meant that the usual constructive ambiguities of Union legislation is even wider than normal. The number of cases brought to the CJEU in the short space of time since 2015 has been significant and inevitably continues to grow apace.

Administration

Distinctions between the appliable inheritance law and the applicable administration law and the fact that both are included within the concept of succession under the Regulation should not be forgotten.

PIL in England & Wales defines administration as relating to such matters as the order of payment of debts, the power to make payments to maintain infant beneficiaries and the power to postpone the sale of assets. Issues regarding the order of application of assets in payment of debts or legacies or the distribution of the net estate to beneficiaries are characterised as matters of inheritance law.

The administration is governed by the law of the state from which the personal representative derives his authority. Under the law of England & Wales, a distinction is made between principal administration and ancillary administration.

Principal administration is administration of the deceased's assets under the authority of the state of the deceased's domicile, whilst ancillary administration is administration under the authority of some other country. This distinction is relevant in relation to the duties of personal representatives and in relation to their obligations in respect of debts. As discussed in chapter 16, administration will generally be governed by one law if there is a valid *professio juris,* but will often be governed by many laws if there is no such valid choice.

Taxation

Whilst taxation is outside the scope of the Regulation, taxation systems on death are inevitably linked to the local succession rights and arrangements. Family members with succession rights are generally taxed more favourably than other beneficiaries. An automatic change of the succession law, will therefore inevitably affect the tax paid as property passes from the deceased to the beneficiaries. Systems such as in the UK that require the appointment of personal representatives, gives a neutral tax role to them. This is not necessarily the case under other taxation systems. S.147 Inheritance Tax Act 1984 deals with Scottish forced heirship claims, but not such claims under other law.

The application of freedom of movement to capital and estate taxation is outside the scope of the Regulation and this book. However, the CJEU has been active on the subject and the two areas may overlap in the future.

CHAPTER FOUR

HABITUAL RESIDENCE

There is no universal definition of habitual residence.

The Law Commission of England and Wales report on domicile[34] pointed out the advantages of habitual residence as a connecting factor in that it is generally easier to establish than domicile because it is less dependent on the mental intention of the person concerned; it is simpler to explain to the layman and hence an easier concept than domicile for both members of the public and officials to use; and it is applicable directly to all persons without the need for a complicated legal rules such as the domicile of dependency to connect a child with a system of law. The United Kingdom has used the concept internally for social security purposes and has its own particular test.

Some EU states such as France, Belgium, Denmark and Luxembourg used residence as a connecting factor for succession law purposes even though nationality was the connecting factor for personal law issues. Often, such residence was defined in a similar manner as for tax residence being for more than six months in any one year, but consideration was given as to questions of the centre of a person's business, social and family life and with an element of intention. France and Belgium called such a connecting factor *domicile,* to be carefully distinguished from domicile in a common law sense.

---

34 Law Commission, Private International Law: Law of Domicile, (Law Com No 168, 1987).

Habitual Residence under Hague Conventions

The various Hague Conventions use the concept of habitual residence frequently.

The Waters Explanatory Report to HccH32[35] states that:[36] 'A person can only have one habitual residence because it is the centre of his living, the place with which he is most closely associated in his pattern of life. For the purpose of determining this place, his family and personal ties are particularly important elements. Intention appears to play a more muted role as an element in habitual residence than it traditionally has done in domicile, and this is why lawyers who are accustomed to working with domicile as a connecting factor hesitate before accepting the term, habitual residence, as an equivalent, but finally accept it as a possible alternative. It is a regular physical presence, enduring for some time, and a clearly stronger association than "ordinary" or "simple" residence of which the *de cujus* may have two or more. However, the manifest hopes and plans of the *de cujus* are also elements that may be legitimately considered by the person who would have to know which State is the habitual residence".

Unlike the European Union, however, there is no universal overriding supreme court to rule on matters relating to a Hague Convention. It is therefore always a matter for individual national courts to provide the local interpretation of a Hague Convention in a particular jurisdiction. There is therefore no enforceable rule that the term habitual residence must have the same meaning in all contracting states or even within contracting states, such as differing parts of the UK for the purposes of the same convention.

Equally, whilst the intention is that all Hague Conventions should provide an interlocking set of rules which do not overlap, but butt snugly

---

35 Available at http://www.hcch.net/upload/expl32e.pdf

36 At page 549, paragraph 51.

up to each other, there does not seem to be any authority that the term must have the same meaning under differing Hague Conventions.

Habitual Residence under EU Legislation

In the EU area of freedom, security and justice, reference to nationality is considered politically inappropriate. Habitual residence, *gewöhnlicher Aufenthalt* in German and *résidence habituelle* in French, has therefore established itself as the EU connecting factor of choice.

For the purposes of each of the various individual EU regulations the term habitual residence has one meaning throughout the European Union and is subject to the defining jurisdiction of the Court of Justice of the European Union. "The need for a uniform application of Community law and the principle of equality require that the terms of a provision of Community law which makes no express reference to the law of the Member States for the purpose of determining its meaning and scope must normally be given an independent and uniform interpretation throughout the Community; that interpretation must take into account the context of the provision and the purpose of the relevant regulations."[37]

Habitual Residence is used as a connecting factor in many EU regulations, such as Brussels II *bis*,[38] the Maintenance Obligations

37 *Ekro* C-327/82 para.11

38 Council Regulation (EC) 2201/2003 concerning jurisdiction and the recognition and enforcement of judgments in matrimonial matters and the matters of parental responsibility, repealing Regulation (EC) No 1347/2000 [2003] OJ L 338/1, Brussels II.

regulation[39] and regulations Rome I,[40] II[41]and III.[42] There is however no specific definition of habitual residence in any of these regulations.

Judge David Hayton[43] defines the issues in relation to habitual residence that require clarification as being:

- What degree of importance is to be given to intention in determining whether residence is habitual?
- How long must residence persist or what quality does it need to have to become habitual?
- Can an individual have more than one habitual residence, in which case how does one determine the dominant habitual residence?
- What weight is to be given to intention and duration in relation to each of a person's personal, social and economic interests, in assessing habitual residence?

However, as stated by AG Sharpston,[44] residence has different functions in EU law. "In certain contexts, it might be used as a criterion for

---

39 Council Regulation (EC) 4/2009 on jurisdiction, applicable law, recognition and enforcement of decisions and cooperation in matters relating to maintenance obligations [2009] OJ L 7/1.

40 Council Regulation (EC) 593/2008 on the law applicable to contractual obligations [2008] OJ L177/6.

41 Council Regulation (EC) 864/2007 on the on the law applicable to non-contractual obligations [2007] OJ L199/40.

42 Council Regulation (EU) No 1259/2010 implementing enhanced cooperation in the area of the law applicable to divorce and legal separation [2012] OJ L/343/10.

43 David Hayton, European Succession Laws (Jordans, 2002)

44 C-456/12 Opinion par. 98

determining the applicable law (for example, in tax law and private international law) and to avoid so-called benefits tourism. Elsewhere, it might be the substance of a right or an element whose absence excludes access to a benefit. In certain contexts, it is expressly defined. In others, it is not. Thus, residence is not a uniform concept in EU law."

The test adopted by CJEU in the case of *Mercredi v Chaffe*[45] decided that the concept of 'habitual residence' for the purposes of Brussels II *bis*, must be interpreted as meaning 'the place which reflects some degree of integration by the child in a social and family environment' in the country concerned. This depends upon numerous factors, including the reasons for the family's stay in the country in question.

In the case of the Succession Regulation, it is clear that the term habitual residence requires an even closer *nexus* than in other EU Regulations. Recital 23 explains "In order to determine the habitual residence, the authority dealing with the succession should make an overall assessment of the circumstances of the life of the deceased during the years preceding his death and at the time of his death, taking account of all relevant factual elements, in particular the duration and regularity of the deceased's presence in the State concerned and the conditions and reasons for that presence. The habitual residence thus determined should reveal a close and stable connection with the State concerned taking into account the specific aims of this Regulation."

The issues in relation to the concept of the habitual residence of a testator and the last habitual residence of a deceased are somewhat different to the habitual residence of a child.

So far, the meaning of habitual residence in the Regulation has only been considered by the CJEU in one case, that of *E.E.*[46] Like all CJEU judgments, what is not stated is important as well as what is stated as

45 C-497/10 PPU [2010] ECR I-14309.

46 C-80/19

unanimously agreed. The opinion of the Attorney General,[47] not being made by a panel unanimously, is a little more forthcoming.

The court noted that while there is no provision in the Regulation that defines the concept of "habitual residence of the deceased at the time of death," useful indications are contained in recitals 23 (above) and 24.

Recital 24 of the Regulation refers to various situations in which it may be difficult to determine habitual residence.

> "In certain cases, determining the deceased's habitual residence may prove complex. Such a case may arise, in particular, where the deceased for professional or economic reasons had gone to live abroad to work there, sometimes for a long time, but had maintained a close and stable connection with his State of origin. In such a case, the deceased could, depending on the circumstances of the case, be considered still to have his habitual residence in his State of origin in which the centre of interests of his family and his social life was located. Other complex cases may arise where the deceased lived in several States alternately or travelled from one State to another without settling permanently in any of them. If the deceased was a national of one of those States or had all his main assets in one of those States, his nationality or the location of those assets could be a special factor in the overall assessment of all the factual circumstances."

The case provides some clarification as to which key factors should be assessed in order to determine the deceased's habitual residence by virtue of these recitals and in line with the objectives of the Regulation. When assessing the deceased's habitual residence at the time of death, a lengthy determination of the circumstances of the deceased's life preceding death should be made.

47 M. Campos Sánchez-Bordona

The CJEU agreed[48] with the opinion of the Attorney General[49] (AG) that for the purposes of the Regulation a person can only have one habitual residence at the time of death, in order to be consistent with the objectives of the Regulation, and that the habitual residence of the deceased must be determined in a single Member State (or presumably, a third State) by the authority dealing with the succession, by an overall assessment of the circumstances of the case.[50]

This view is not without its critics who would question whether the concept of habitual residence is inherently contrary to the notion of EU citizenship. An EU citizen being limited to habitual residence in just one Member State might be seen as in breach of the TEU.

The AG's opinion made various other points:[51]

> Although reference to the definition of habitual residence used in other EU Regulations can be made, recital 23 makes it clear that for the purposes of the Regulation the habitual residence must reveal a close and stable link with a State, which must be assessed in the light of *the specific aims of the Regulation*, listed in recital 7.
>
> Practitioners must therefore establish the deceased's last habitual residence with these provisions in mind, and in the light of the guidance given in the Regulation itself, and only rely on other guidance on an ancillary basis.
>
> Habitual residence must be determined on the basis of a general assessment of the circumstances of the deceased's life during the

48 At para.41 and referred to the judgments of *Kubicka*, C-218/16, point 57, and *Oberle*, C-20/17, points 53 to 55

49 At para.42

50 Para.

51 At paras.47 - 51

years preceding his death and at the time of his death.

The authority with jurisdiction must gather all relevant and legally admissible evidence. In that context, mere declarations by persons with an interest in the succession which are mutually corroborative and are made before an authority dealing with the succession that does not perform judicial functions are not sufficient to establish the deceased's habitual residence.

The combination of factual elements relating to the deceased's life, as referred to in recital 23, will form the basis for deciding which of the situations envisaged in that and the recital 24 reflect the circumstances of a particular deceased person.

The AG then[52] divided cross border cases between those that do have a close and stable connection with a State and those other cases in which the deceased had not been present in any particular State on a regular and long-term basis.

In the first category both the objective factors relating to the duration and regularity of the deceased's presence in a State and the subjective factors being the circumstances of and reasons for his presence there, should reveal in and of themselves the existence of a 'close and stable connection' with that State.

The AG did not think any immediate inference can be drawn from the deceased's residence for tax or marital purposes; these factors will fall to be examined, along with all other relevant evidence, as part of an overall assessment. Whilst *stability* is what is looked for at this initial stage of the analysis, once this has been confirmed, no further definitive inferences should be drawn from it in relation to the deceased's habitual residence. It may also be necessary to assess the circumstances warranting such residence, so as to identify the place where his interests were habitually managed. In particular, whether the deceased was employed (gainfully or

52 Paras. 52 – 58

otherwise) and, if so, where, for how long and under what type of contract (if any), whether or not he had any permanent accommodation, what his home background and social circles were, where he received medical treatment, which authority was responsible for any related costs … and so on.

Although EU legislation gives priority to the criterion of habitual residence, the increasing mobility of individuals cannot be ignored. Therefore the length of time a person spends in a Member State is not, in itself, a decisive criterion: what matters is to examine each case in such a way as to ascertain whether other evidence, relating to the person's family and his social connections with, and proximity to, the place in question, corroborates the result indicated by the time factor.

The second situation is described in recital 24 of the Regulation and covers cases in which there is no indication of the deceased having been present in a particular State on a regular and long-term basis. There are two possible reasons for this:

- The person concerned may have moved abroad as a matter of professional choice, although without having changed the 'centre of interests of his family and social life'.

- It may also be the case that the deceased split his life between a number of States without establishing a stable connection with any of them.

In those scenarios, a personal consideration (the deceased's nationality) or an economic one (the location of his principal assets) may have a particular bearing on the overall assessment of all the factual circumstances.

In the AG's view, the CJEU should emphasise that the deceased's nationality and the location of his assets are *ancillary* determiners of habitual residence. In other words, a combined examination of the factual elements relating to the stability of the deceased's situation and the reasons for it will serve to determine whether his situation is 'complex', to use the terminology of recital 24 itself.

Any recourse to the deceased's nationality and the location of his principal assets should only be after this prior detailed examination and by way of exception to ensure legal certainty within the scheme established by the Regulation.

The Regulation "must be interpreted in the sense that it falls within the concept of "transferring a cross-border succession" to a situation in which the deceased, a national of one Member State, resided in another Member State at the time of his death, but had not severed his ties with the first of those Member States, in which the assets comprising his estate are located, while his successors have their residence in those two Member States. The last habitual residence of the deceased, within the meaning of this regulation, must be fixed by the authority seized of the estate in only one of those Member States."[53]

As discussed in chapter 6, art.2 underlines the fact that the Regulation only applies if a cross-border element is involved in the succession. At para.42 the court in *E.E.* held that, it is necessary to assess whether the estate is a cross border one because of the location of another element relating to it in a different state from that of the deceased's last habitual residence and that a succession has cross-border elements when it includes property located in several Member States and, in particular, in a different state from that of the deceased's last residence.[54] In addition, the Regulation addresses, in a non-exhaustive way, other circumstances which may reveal the existence of an estate involving several Member States. Unsurprisingly, the CJEU found that the facts in *E.E.* did make it a cross border one to which the Regulation applied.

---

53 Para.45

54 The Court referred to *Oberle*, C-20/17, para. 32

The question of the applicable law under art.21.1 and the issues relating to the exception of a "manifestly more close connection" in art.21.2 which is a matter for the court with jurisdiction, are considered in chapter 7.

CHAPTER FIVE

STRUCTURE OF THE REGULATION

Constructive ambiguity is a term often credited to Henry Kissinger and also often discredited as a fudge that kicks problems down the road. However, every piece of European Union legislation is a pragmatic compromise. In order for it to work, an element of uncertainty is inevitable for it to be broad enough to apply across its 25/27 different legal systems and its 24 languages. Uncertainties are only resolved as and when they reach the CJEU.

The Regulation was unusual in being so far reaching, ambitious and of such a broad scope. It is natural that the drafters of the Regulation should first look to the Brussels I Regulation[55] as a model, but many aspects of the Hague Convention of 1 August 1989 on the Law Applicable to Succession to the Estates of Deceased Persons[56] (HccH 32) were also used, even though HccH 32 had only been ratified by the Netherlands and had never come into force. Whilst the Brussels I Regulation was available in all of the official languages of the European Union, HccH 32 was only available in French and English although translations in Dutch,

---

55 COUNCIL REGULATION (EC) No 44/2001 of 22 December 2000 on jurisdiction and the recognition and enforcement of judgments in civil and commercial matters https://eur-lex.europa.eu/legal-content/EN/TXT/PDF/?uri=CELEX:32001R0044&from=EN replaced by Brussels I *bis* REGULATION (EU) No 1215/2012 OF THE EUROPEAN PARLIAMENT AND OF THE COUNCIL of 12 December 2012 on jurisdiction and the recognition and enforcement of judgments in civil and commercial matters (recast) https://eur-lex.europa.eu/LexUriServ/LexUriServ.do?uri=OJ:L:2012:351:0001:0032:en:PDF

56 https://www.hcch.net/en/instruments/conventions/full-text/?cid=62

German and Polish have been made. Some of the difficulties between different linguistic versions of the Regulation stem from the initial differences between the French and English versions of HccH 32.

83 recitals begin the Regulation with some nine and a half initial pages of them setting out the Regulation's broad landscape. As explained at point 10 in the EUR-Lex Joint Practical Guide for drafting legislation,[57] "the purpose of the recitals is to set out concise reasons for the chief provisions of the enacting terms, without reproducing or paraphrasing them. They shall not contain normative provisions or political exhortations." However, some of the recitals in the Regulation are somewhat opaque and do not always add to clarity or explain all of the enacting terms, which are the subsequent articles.

The Regulation in the same manner as other EU Regulations is divided into chapters dealing with separate topics of Private International Law.

- Chapter I (Arts.1 to 3) covers Scope, Exclusions and Definitions.

- Chapter II (Arts.4 to 19) deals with Jurisdiction, which is usually given to the state of the last habitual residence.

- Chapter III (Arts.20 to 38) relates to Applicable Law which is to be that of the state of the last habitual residence, but with the ability for the testator specifically to choose the law of nationality in its place, the professio juris. Renvoi is partially abolished. The Chapter also deals with questions as to capacity and validity of Wills and Succession Agreements ("Dispositions of Property upon Death")

[57] http://eur-lex.europa.eu/content/pdf/techleg/joint-practical-guide-2013-en.pdf

- Chapter IV (Arts.39 to 58) deals with Recognition, Enforceability and Enforcement

- Chapter V (Arts.59 to 61) affects Authentic Instruments and Court Settlements

- Chapter VI (Arts.62 to 73) concerns the European Certificate of Succession

- Chapter VII (Arts.74 to 84) deals with General and Final Provisions.

The Regulation has been published in all the 24 official languages of the European Union:[58] Bulgarian, Croatian, Czech, Danish, Dutch, English, Estonian, Finnish, French, German, Greek, Hungarian, Irish, Italian, Latvian, Lithuanian, Maltese, Polish, Portuguese, Romanian, Slovak, Slovenian, Spanish and Swedish. Three of these 24 (English, French and German) have the higher status of "procedural" languages of the European Commission (whilst the Parliament uses all official languages). However, for the purposes of interpreting legislation each language version is of equal weight.

The English version of the original draft was translated from the French version, and inevitably there were some translation and transposition issues, but the Regulation has rectified many, but not all of these linguistic problems.

As discussed further in the next chapter, the linguistic issues are particularly acute in art.1 in relation to the scope of the Regulation. Article 1.1 in the English version states that, "This Regulation shall apply to succession to the estates of deceased persons." Mirroring the linguistic differences in HccH32, the French and German versions however do not

58 https://eur-lex.europa.eu/legal-content/EN/TXT/?uri=CELEX%3A32012R0650

refer to "an estate", but say, "Le présent règlement s'applique aux successions à cause de mort", and "Diese Verordnung ist auf die Rechtsnachfolge von Todes wegen anzuwenden".

For Greek scholars, "O παρών κανονισμός εφαρμόζεται στις κληρονομικές διαδοχές" is straightforward. Unsurprisingly, the Italian, "Il presente regolamento si applica alle successioni a causa di morte", and the Portuguese, "O presente regulamento é aplicável às sucessões por morte", follow the French version. The Dutch, "Deze verordening is van toepassing op de erfopvolging in de nalatenschappen van overleden personen", and the Gaelic, "Beidh feidhm ag an Rialachán seo maidir le comharbas ar eastáit daoine éagtha" follow the English, whilst the Maltese version refers to both succession and patrimony of a deceased person, "Dan ir-Regolament għandu japplika għas-suċċessjoni għall-patrimonji tad-deċeduti".

The EU asserts that it is in favour of linguistic diversity. This principle is enshrined in the EU Charter of Fundamental Rights (article 22) and in the Treaty on European Union (article 3(3) TEU).

In addition, the CJEU has stated that "a purely literal interpretation of one or more language versions of a multilingual text of European Union law, to the exclusion of the others, cannot, however, prevail since the uniform application of European Union rules requires that they be interpreted, inter alia, in the light of the versions drawn up in all the languages (see, to that effect, Jany and Others, C 268/99, paragraph 47 and the case-law cited, and Commission v Spain, C 189/11, paragraph 56 and the case-law cited). Where there is divergence between the language versions of a European Union text, the provision in question must be interpreted by reference to the general scheme and purpose of the rules of which it forms part (see, to that effect, ZVK, C-300/05, paragraph 16 and the case-law cited; Haasová, C-22/12, paragraph 48; and Drozdovs, C 277/12, paragraph 39).[59]

It is not certain as to how to resolve the linguistic diversity, particularly of art.1, in favour of a single meaning but it is clear that a definition of "Succession" is to be inferred, in its broadest sense whereas exclusions, by contrast, should be interpreted in their narrower sense.

Other linguistic issues are, for example, the term "beneficiary" which is used to include both "heirs" (or residuary beneficiaries) and "legatees" but the terms are not necessarily clearly distinguished, since under some laws legatees merely have a claim against heirs or administrators whilst in others they may have a right in rem to an asset.[60]

This book is written for readers practising in states that are not themselves bound by the Regulation and for this reason it contains limited commentary on matters of jurisdiction, recognition and enforcement, authentic instruments and the European Certificate of Succession dealt with in Chapters II, IV, V and VI of the Regulation, which will not directly affect such third States, although practitioners will need to be aware of the various provisions.

The boundaries between succession rights and property rights are often in different places under different systems and this is further explored in Chapter 18. Each Member State will always have its own individual perspective on the Regulation and the way its systems of inheritance and its historic rules of private international law interact with the Regulation. Although as the years pass and CJEU issues more decisions, the differences in the ways different Member States treat the Regulation may diminish, they will never completely disappear.

---

59 C-162/13 of September 4, 2014, Damijan Vnuk v Zavarovalnica Triglav d.d. at para. 46.

60 Recital 47

CHAPTER SIX

SCOPE, APPLICATION, EXCLUSIONS AND DEFINITIONS – CHAPTER I OF THE REGULATION

Scope

The relationship between arts.1, 2, 3 and 23 is at the heart of an understanding of the Regulation.

Article 1 defines the scope of the Regulation and is key to its interpretation. It cannot be said too often, that if the Regulation does not apply, none of the other articles apply. Thus, if a matter is outside the scope of the Regulation, then none of the other parts of the Regulation can apply. For example, other parts of the Regulation may refer to matters such as tax, but since revenue matters are outside the scope of the Regulation, no part of the Regulation can affect tax directly.

Article 2 underlines the fact that the Regulation only applies to cross border successions and art.3 defines some, but not all, important concepts.

Article 23 deals with the scope of the applicable succession law within the framework of the Regulation. The scope of the applicable law under art.23, will not limit other portions of the Regulation. Even though a matter may not be governed by the applicable law under art.23, it may still be a matter governed by the Regulation and therefore subject to issues of jurisdiction, recognition, enforceability and enforcement under the law of the state of the jurisdiction as opposed to that of the state of the applicable law. This is considered further in chapter 7.

The *Acquis* or body of law of the EU, aims to build a series of regulations in such a way that a category of law dealt with under one regulation is excluded from another. Thus, reference can be made to other regulations that govern such categories excluded from the Regulation, to assist in understanding the definitions of scope and the various exclusions of the Regulation itself. The CJEU has held that interpretation of EU Regulations requires independent, community wide, autonomous principles which are required in order to ensure the equal and uniform operation of a regulation.[61]

The Regulation applies to succession to the estates of deceased persons.[62] This simple statement seems self-obvious, but as discussed in chapter 5 contains many conundrums. The French and German versions do not refer to "an estate", but state, "*Le présent règlement s'applique aux successions à cause de mort*", and "*Diese Verordnung ist auf die Rechtsnachfolge von Todes wegen anzuwenden*". "Succession" is defined in art.3, but not "estate".

It is uncertain as to how to resolve this linguistic diversity in favour of a single meaning, but it is clear that the CJEU will look to the overriding purpose of the Regulation. The Regulation was produced under article 81 of the TFEU relating to judicial co-operation and its purposes set out in recitals 1 to 9 of the Regulation include the proper functioning of the internal market and the extension of mutual recognition to areas of law such as succession and wills that are essential to everyday life. Accordingly, and as discussed below in relation to art.3.1(a), it is believed that a broad definition of "Succession" is to be inferred.

---

61 C-29/76 in relation to the Brussels I *bis* Regulation.

62 Art.1.1

Exclusions

Under art.1.1 the Regulation is not to apply to revenue, customs or administrative matters. Notwithstanding that these matters are outside its scope, the Regulation does of course have considerable effect on tax matters, since change to the applicable law and thus changes to the relevant heirs or beneficiaries will consequentially result in different tax effects. Article 1.2 sets out further exclusions to which the Regulation will not apply.

In the case of *Winkler v Shamoon*[63] there is a helpful reminder of the CJEU decision in *German Graphics Graphische Maschinen GmbH v van der Schee*[64] that exclusions should be interpreted narrowly, not broadly. The exclusions in art.1.2(a)-(l) should be presumed to be exhaustive and no further exclusions are to be permitted, whereas the scope of the applicable law defined under art.23 refers to the law governing "in particular" and the list in paragraphs (a) to (j) of art.23 is therefore not exhaustive.

Specified Exclusions

Article 1.2 contains twelve specified categories of excluded matters. Only two of the categories are covered by other EU regulations; (d) matrimonial and partnership property regimes[65] which is dealt with in chapter 13 and (e) covering maintenance obligations[66] other than those arising on death.

63 [2016] EWHC 217 Ch at para. 50.

64 C-292/08

65 Which are within the scope of enhanced co-operation regulations (EU) 2016/1103 and 2016/1104.

66 Within the scope of regulation (EC) 4/2009 and HccH39

The other categories are a mixed bag, some of which might be the subject of future EU regulations, but many of which will not.

(a) Status of Persons and Relationships

The term 'family relationships' is not defined, but the phrase 'relationships deemed by the law applicable to such relationships to have comparable effects' is presumably intended to include all parent and child relationships including adoption and surrogacy. Similarly, relationships comparable with marriage should include all officially recognized forms of union, whether between persons of the same sex or of mixed sex. These would include relationships such as civil partnerships in the United Kingdom or Ireland.

The status and validity of a particular family relationship, will not be a matter within the scope of the Regulation. Each Member State will apply its own PIL and apply its individual national rules on these matters.

In such cases although the Regulation will govern the jurisdiction and the applicable law for a succession, there will be circumstances in which differing natural persons may qualify as heirs according to the individual relevant law of a Member State on the validity or otherwise of the relationship.

Questions of public policy may however, intrude on these matters and are considered in chapter 24.

(b) Legal capacity of persons

This exclusion which is specifically without prejudice to arts.23.2 and 26, should be contrasted with the HccH32 which excludes the capacity to dispose of property upon death in article 1(2)(b).

Some legal systems classify matters of fraud, mistake, undue influence etc, as being related to capacity. However, since art.26 makes it clear that for the purposes of making a DoPuD under the Regulation these are classified as matters of substantial validity, it is presumed that art.1.2(b) would be construed restrictively and not exclude these.

Similarly, art.23.1(c) includes the capacity to inherit within the applicable succession law. The general capacity to inherit will be within the scope of the Regulation, whilst the specific capacity of a particular individual, will not.

(c) The disappearance, absence or presumed death of a natural person

There is an ICCS[67] Convention no.10 (the Athens Convention) of 14 September 1966 that applies if the death of a missing person can be regarded as certain, but although it has been signed by France and Switzerland, it has only entered into force in Greece, the Netherlands, Portugal, Spain and Turkey.

There are however no conventions in relation to missing persons whose deaths are not certain.

The Presumption of Death Act 2013 changed the law in England & Wales, and permits an application to court for a declaration to be made if a person who is missing has not known to be alive for at least 7 years. The same period applies in Scotland under the Presumption of Death (Scotland) Act 1977. However, very different periods can apply in other states. In Italy, the period can be 20 years; in France, it can be 10 years.

The Council of Europe produced a Recommendation, CM/Rec (2009) 12, in 2009 which suggested that the waiting period should be 7 years at most, but this has not yet produced significant change in the laws of Member States.

The effects of a person going missing can be traumatic on the family left behind. It is not unusual for another member of the family to grieve and die. The succession entitlements of the estates of either will differ

67 Details of the ICCS are in chapter 1

depending on the order of death. The succession in different states will therefore be different and the place of the assets will then affect who is entitled, since the deemed date of death will depend upon the local law rather than the succession law applicable under the Regulation.

(d) matrimonial and partnership property regimes

This exclusion is dealt with in chapter 13.

(e) maintenance obligations

Maintenance obligations arising from a family relationship, parentage, marriage or affinity are within the scope of regulation (EC) 4/2009 and HccH39. These include for example the obligation of children to maintain their parents under some systems.

The exclusion will not extend to obligations arising on death, which refers to obligations to and therefore the succession rights of family members. Some systems classify clawback as a form of maintenance, and it is clear that this exclusion does not extend to clawback, which is considered in chapter 18.

(f) formal validity of DoPuDs made orally

This exclusion is considered in chapter 15. The reference in art.27 to DoPuDs made in writing is hoped to be superfluous, since the formal validity of oral DoPuDs is already outside the scope of the Regulation. HccH32 applies to agreements as to succession that are solely created in writing. HccH11 by contrast can apply to oral wills.

(g) Property rights passing otherwise than by succession

The boundaries between succession law and the transfer of property rights is murky and difficult. Death automatically transfers property, since the owner is no more. This exclusion is based on HccH32 article 1.2(d). Paragraph 46 of the Waters Report lists many different varieties of will substitutes which would all be excluded.

Paragraph 4.1 of the Explanatory Memorandum states that "the exclusion of rights and properties created or transferred other than by means of succession to the estates of deceased persons covers not only the forms of joint property [joint tenancy] known under common law, but also all forms of gifts under civil law."

Thus, none of the Regulation applies to property passing by survivorship, if that is property passing otherwise than by succession. It is here that linguistic issues referred to before in chapter 1 are particularly acute, since the exclusion is "without prejudice to point (i) of art.23.2".

The very important question as to whether or not and in what circumstances gifts to heirs and also to third parties can be subject to clawback and may or may not be within the scope of the Regulation is considered in chapter 18.

(h) Property rights in companies

(i) Dissolution and merger of companies

These two exclusions might be thought to be somewhat redundant. However, art.1.2(h) should be borne in mind when considering the special provisions of art.30 limiting the transfer of particular entities, considered in chapter 7, since if they relate to the constitution of an entity, then they may be outside the scope of the Regulation in any event.

(j) Creation, administration and dissolution of trusts

As the Explanatory Report states at 4.1 "The exception envisaged for trusts is not an obstacle to the application to succession of the law governing it on the basis of this Regulation." The exclusion is limited and the applicable succession law will govern the transmission of property and determination of beneficiaries in relation to trusts created on death under that law.

The exclusion merely excludes the functioning of the trust from the scope of the Regulation.

(k) Nature of rights in rem

The Explanatory Report states "that the Regulation applies to the acquisition of a right in rem relating to inherited property, but not to the content of such a right. The Regulation does not affect the "numerus clausus" of property law in the Member States, the classification of property and rights, and the determination of the prerogatives of the holder of such rights. As a consequence, it is not, in principle, valid to establish a right in rem without knowing the law of the place in which the property is located. The law on succession cannot lead to the introduction in the State in which the property is located of a property law clause, or the stripping of such clause, without the knowledge of the State. For example, usufruct cannot be introduced in a State which does not recognise it. However, this exception does not apply to the transfer of a right in rem recognised by the Member State in which the inherited property is located." The boundaries between succession law and property rights are extremely varied and difficult and are considered in chapter 3.

(l) Recording of property rights in registers

The fact that the Explanatory Report is terse on this issue, whilst there a number of long relevant recitals, indicates the political difficulties that shaped the negotiation of this exclusion.

Recital 18 elaborates on the issue of recording in a register at some considerable length. "'The requirements for the recording in a register of a right in immovable or movable property should be excluded for the scope of this Regulation. It should therefore be the law of the Member State in which the register is kept (for immovable property, the *lex rei sitae*) which determines under what legal conditions and how the recording must be carried out and which authorities, such as land registers or notaries, are in charge of checking that all requirements are met and that the documentation presented or established is sufficient or contains the necessary information. In particular, the authorities may check that the right of the deceased to the succession property mentioned in the document presented for registration is a right which is recorded as such in the register or which is otherwise demonstrated in accordance with the law of the Member State in which the register is kept. In order to avoid duplication of documents, the registration authorities should accept such documents drawn up in another Member State by the competent authorities whose circulation is provided for by this Regulation, in particular, the European Certificate of Succession issued under this regulation should constitute a valid document for the recording of succession property in a register of a Member State. This should not preclude the authorities involved in the registration from asking the person applying for registration to provide such additional information, or to present such additional documents as are required under the law of the Member State in which the register is kept, for instance information or documents relating to the payment of revenue. The competent authority may indicate to the person applying for registration how the missing information or documents can be provided."

This issue was considered by the CJEU in *RJR v Registru Centras*[68] which is dealt with in Chapter 19.

Revenue matters are in any event outside the scope of the Regulation by virtue of art.1(1), so that reference to them in the recital is somewhat superfluous.

Recital 19 deals with the exclusion of the effects of the recording of a right in a register. "'It should therefore be the law of the Member State in which the register is kept which determines whether the recording is, for instance, declaratory or constitutive in effect. Thus, where, for example, the acquisition of a right in immovable property requires a

68 C-354/21

recording in a register under the law of the Member State in which the register is kept in order to ensure the *erga omnes* effect of registers or to protect legal transactions, the moment of such acquisition should be governed by the law of that Member State."

Although the exclusions in (k) and (l) are not stated to be without prejudice to the doctrine of adaptation referred to in recital 16, adaptation is not excluded from the scope of the Regulation. These aspects and the CJEU decision in *Kubicka*[69] are considered in chapter 19.

Insolvent Estates

Article 76 of the Regulation should not be forgotten in the context of insolvency. As recommended in the Max Planck report, art.76 excludes the application of the Regulation to the Insolvency Regulation 1346/2000 so that the Insolvency Regulation takes precedence.

Cross-Border Successions Only

Article 2 states that the Regulation shall not affect the competence of the individual Member States to deal with matters of succession. This appears to be somewhat superfluous, save that it underlines the fact that the Regulation deals with the private international law of succession and that absent any cross border PIL question, the jurisdiction of each of the Member States continue unaffected by the Regulation. There is no reference to art.2 in the Explanatory Report or in a recital.

The CJEU has noted[70] that the Regulation was adopted on the basis of article 81, para.2, TFUE, which only covers civil matters with a cross-border impact. Article 2 therefore merely confirms this point that the Regulation cannot affect matters without a cross-border element.

69 C-218/16

70 *E.E.* C-80/19 at para. 34

The case of *Hantoch*[71] makes it clear that the cross-border element must exist at the time of death, but that the Regulation continues to apply even if the cross-border element ceases to exist some time after death.

Entry into force and application

The Regulation entered into force on 17 August 2012 but did not become fully effective until 17 August 2015 and therefore only applies to the successions of persons dying after 16 August 2015. Some administrative provisions entered into force earlier as set out in chapter 8. The transitional provisions of art.83 are considered in chapter 15.

Definitions

Art.3 sets out the definitions of some of the terms used in the Regulation and as described above in relation to scope the CJEU has held that interpretation of EU Regulations requires independent, community wide, autonomous principles.[72] Thus even in circumstances, when the forum court applies its own local law, regard must be had to the autonomous interpretation of the terms and definitions set out in the Regulation, provided that the matter is within its scope.

Succession

HccH32 did not define "succession", but paragraph 39 of the Waters Report makes it clear that the term concerns devolution, but excludes the transmission of assets. In the Regulation, "succession" has a much broader meaning and is defined as meaning "succession to the estate of a deceased person and covers all forms of transfer of assets, rights and obligations by reason of death, whether by way of a voluntary transfer under a disposition of property upon death or a transfer through intestate

---

[71] C-291/23

[72] For example, C-29/76 in relation to the Brussels I *bis* Regulation.

succession" and thus including both devolution and some aspects of transmission.

The term "estate" is not defined. The broad definition of succession in art.3.1(a), however, indicates that "estate" is to be given a very broad meaning indeed.

Recital 9 confirms that the Regulation is wide ranging and "includes all civil-law aspects of succession, namely all forms of transfer of assets, rights and obligations, by reason of death, whether by way of a voluntary transfer under a disposition of property on death or a transfer on intestate succession."[73]

Paragraph 4.1 of the Explanatory Report, states that 'the concept of "succession" must be interpreted in an autonomous manner and encompasses all the elements of a succession, in particular its handover, administration and liquidation', but of course, definitions will only apply in circumstances in which the Regulation itself applies. This will not be the case, in relation to matters outside its scope. Thus, this definition of "succession" must exclude matters such as property rights excluded by reason of art.1.2(g).

Agreement as to succession, Joint Will and Disposition of Property upon Death

These and their definitions under art.3.1(b)-(d) are considered in chapter 15.

Decision, Court Settlement, Authentic Instrument and Court

These and their definitions under arts.3.1(g)-(i) and 3.2 are considered in chapter 11.

[73] This recital is clearly based upon the definition of succession from paragraph 28 of the Waters Report.

Member State of origin and Member State of enforcement

These are defined under arts.3.1(e)-(f) and are fairly self-obvious and are considered in chapter 10.

Matters Not Defined in the Regulation

Some terms, such as "estate" whilst not defined will usually be straightforward to interpret. Others, such as "Member State" and "Habitual Residence" were subject to lengthy discussions during the drafting and legislative process. There is no definition of "Habitual Residence" in the Regulation, but recitals 23 and 24 give guidance as to its interpretation and these and the issues involved with that term are considered in chapter 4.

Member State and third State

The definition of "Member State" was somewhat problematic in theory, but probably not in practice. Now that the United Kingdom has ceased to be treated as a Member State from 1 January 2021, this issue is only still relevant for Ireland and Denmark.

The Treaty on the Functioning of the European Union indicates that a third country is one that is not a Member State[74] whilst the expression Member State includes all Member States that are parties to the EU Treaties.

As set out in Recitals 82 and 83, Denmark and Ireland (and the United Kingdom prior to 1 January 2021) are Member States that are not bound by or subject to the application of the Regulation. In these recitals, Denmark, Ireland and the United Kingdom are referred to as Member States, but there is no specific definition of "Member State" or "third State" in the Regulation.

---

74 See for example article 63 of the TFEU.

The final line of the Regulation: "This Regulation shall be binding in its entirety and directly applicable on the Member States in accordance with the Treaties" can certainly be interpreted as including those three states as Member States. Others argue that reference in the final sentence of Recital 82 to "the United Kingdom and Ireland", rather than to "those Member States" is an indication that they are not to be regarded as such for the purposes of the Regulation.

By virtue of Protocols 21 and 22 to the TEU, Ireland and Denmark will not be bound by or subject to the application of the Regulation, but other Member States do not have the benefit of equivalent protocols to those of Protocols 21 or 22 and therefore the Regulation will bind all of those Member States.

If it had been wished to exclude the three states from the definition of Member State, it would have been perfectly feasible to do so.

The original form of the draft Regulation as proposed by the Commission,[75] included a provision at art.1.2, which stated that "In this Regulation 'Member State' means all the Member States with the exception of Denmark [the United Kingdom and Ireland]." This provision has not survived the legislative process and does not appear in the Regulation.

In many EU Regulations, such a definition has been included, restricting the definition of a Member State to those that are bound by the specific Regulation. In the Brussels I Regulation, for example, art.1.3 [now amended in Brussels I bis Regulation] defined "the term 'Member State' as meaning Member States with the exception of Denmark." Similarly, in the Rome I Regulation, art.1.4 states that "In this Regulation, the term 'Member State' shall mean Member States to which this Regulation applies. However, in art.3(4) and art.7 the term shall mean all the

[75] COM (2009) 154

Member States", and the Maintenance Obligations Regulation[76] specifically defines in art.1.2 that "In this Regulation, the term 'Member State' shall mean Member States to which this Regulation applies".

The most similar equivalent example to the Regulation is perhaps that of the Insolvency Regulation[77] which applies to all Member States, other than Denmark. In that regulation there is also no definition excluding Denmark from the definition of Member State. The external evaluation of the Insolvency Regulation[78] refers in passing to Denmark as being a third State without any authority for such a reference. The CJEU decision in *Seagon v Deko Marty*[79] related to issues involving Germany and Belgium. The Swedish Supreme Court decision in *Siv Ing Benum AS v Kinovox-Benum AB*[80] to issues involving Sweden and Norway and the application of the Nordic 1933 Treaty, but these do not directly address the issue. It would seem that the Swedish Supreme Court was indicating that Denmark may not be a third State.

It may therefore be argued that even though Denmark and Ireland are not bound by or subject to provisions of the Regulation, the definition of Member State in the Regulation does still include Denmark and Ireland, and that therefore the definition of a third State also excludes Denmark and Ireland.

Many opinions from the EU Institutions and national governments support the view that it was intended that non-participating Member States should not be regarded as within the definition of "Member State" in the Regulation. However, any decision on the question will be subject

---

[76] (EC) No 4/2009 of 18 December 2008

[77] (EU) No 1346/2000

[78] JUST/2011/JCIV/PR/0049/A4

[79] C-339/07

[80] Ö 743-11 of 31 January 2013

to review by the Court of Justice of the EU ("CJEU") and may depend upon the political climate at that time.

In the case of *VA and ZA v TP*[81] dealt with in chapter 9, CJEU made it clear that the United Kingdom in 2015 was not a Member State for the purposes of arts. 4 and 19.

Practitioners should be aware that the courts of most Member States are likely to regard Ireland and Denmark, as third States for all purposes of the Regulation.

It has been argued that including all Member States within the definition would create an unfair position as between Member States. It could, however, also be argued that it could be a matter of European policy, that the succession law of Member States should be recognised and enforced throughout the EU whether or not individual Member States are bound by the Regulation.

For most purposes, there is no particular confusion since Denmark and Ireland are not bound by the Regulation or subject to its application. The main point of uncertainty relates to the question of *renvoi*. Article 34.1 only applies to third States. The implication, therefore, is that it does not apply to Member States not bound by the Regulation and that therefore is to be no *renvoi* from Denmark or Ireland to other Member States, but the point is not clear. Article 34.2 would seem to apply in all circumstances, so that a choice of law under art.22 will certainly be a choice of the internal law with no *renvoi*.

If a French domiciled person died habitually resident in Ireland, it could be argued that *renvoi* under Irish PIL back to France did not apply under art.34 and that therefore France should apply the internal law of Ireland and none of its PIL. In order to avoid uncertainty, however, individuals with connections with Denmark or Ireland and whose successions might be subject to *renvoi* back to Member States subject to the Regulation,

---

81 C-645/20

should consider making a choice of applicable law under art.22, where available, in order to avoid such uncertainty.

Any reference to a Member State or to a third State, should therefore be considered carefully and the distinctions between participating and non-participating Member States also fully thought through.

CHAPTER SEVEN

APPLICABLE LAW – CHAPTER III OF THE REGULATION

Chapter III of the Regulation deals with questions that relate to the applicable succession law and much of it is based on HccH32.

By art.21.1 of the Regulation, unless otherwise provided, the law applicable to the succession shall be that of the deceased's habitual residence at the time of death, subject to the more closely connected escape clause of art.21.2 (and subject to a contrary choice under art.22 and to any *renvoi* issues under art.34) and is to apply to the whole of the succession. The intention is that usually the jurisdiction under art.4 and the applicable law under art.21 will coincide. Article 20 makes it clear that unlike art.4 which only gives jurisdiction to a Member State, art.21 applies whether or not the applicable law is the law of a Member State. Distinctions between movable and immovable are often removed. *Renvoi* is partially abolished.

"Unless otherwise provided" refers to the escape clause of art.21.2 or to the *renvoi* provisions of art.34. Also as discussed below, many matters within the scope of the Regulation are not necessarily governed by the applicable succession law.

The intention behind the Regulation will always be the primary driver behind any CJEU decision. A valid choice of law should bring with it the whole of that law, so far as it relates to those matters that are within the scope of the applicable succession law. As set out in Recital 37, "For reasons of legal certainty and in order to avoid the fragmentation of the succession, that law should govern the succession as a whole...irrespective of the nature of the assets and regardless of whether the assets are located in another Member State or in a third State". This fact is often uncomfortable for some systems and practitioners to accept.

Escape Clause

Art.21.2 provides an exception to the general habitual residence rule, of a manifestly more close connection. Recital 25 makes it clear that this "should not be resorted to as a subsidiary connecting factor whenever the determination of the habitual residence of the deceased at the time of death proves complex."

This provision was considered by CJEU in the case of *E.E.* Para. 59 of the Opinion of the AG states "I would point out, lastly, that, so far as concerns establishing the applicable law, recital 25 onwards of the Regulation prohibits the use as a subsidiary connecting factor of the criterion of the deceased's 'manifestly closest connection' with a legal system other than that of the place of his last habitual residence, even in cases where determining habitual residence proves complex. This makes it clear, in my opinion, that there is no getting out of identifying a place of habitual residence, however difficult this may be."

Recital 25 of the Regulation, and confirmed by the AG in para.25 of the Opinion, states that a typical situation falling under "manifestly closest connection" is when the deceased moved to their new habitual residence fairly recently before their death. With respect, and alternatively, this may indicate that the new residence has not yet become habitual. CJEU has not yet identified any specific elements for the determination of the exceptional "manifestly closest connection" criterion, but para.45 of the judgment indicates that the exceptional use of the "manifestly closest connection" criterion is, however, left to the judicial discretion of the national court first seised.

Applicable Law

Article 21.1 states that, unless otherwise provided, the applicable law is to govern the succession as a whole. Recital 42 indicates that this is to be from its opening to the final transfer of the ownership to the assets to the beneficiaries or heirs. Article 23.2 sets out a goodly number of specific matters governed "in particular" by the applicable law. The use of the phrase "in particular" indicates that the list is not exhaustive.

The particular matters specified include the opening of the succession, the determination of the beneficiaries and their respective shares, capacity to inherit, disinheritance and disqualification by conduct, the transfer of the assets, rights and obligations making up the estate to the legatees, the powers of heirs and executors and administrators, the liability for debts, the disposable part of the estate, the reserved shares and other restrictions on the disposing of property on death as well as claims which persons close to the deceased may have against the estate or the heirs, obligations to restore or account for gifts and the sharing out of the estate.

The powers of executors and administrators are considered in chapter 16, the liability for debts in chapter 17 and the "obligation to restore or account for gifts, advancements or legacies when determining the shares of the different beneficiaries" in chapter 18.

It should be remembered that there can easily be particular matters not governed by the applicable law. The obvious example is that of a succession agreement which can be governed by the law under which it was prepared, provided that this meets with the requirements of arts.25 and 27. The definition of an "agreement as to succession" under art.3.1(c) may well include a broad range of such agreements such as the doctrines of mutual wills and of proprietary estoppel under the laws of England and Wales or other common law jurisdictions, but it must be remembered that the Succession Regulation excludes from its scope the formal validity of oral DoPuDs under art.1.2(f), but the admissibility, substantive validity and binding effects of such oral Agreements as to Succession, will still be governed by art.25. Whether a DoPuD is made in writing or merely evidenced in writing may prove interesting.

Thus, the entire succession of a person who dies habitually resident in, for example Spain, will be governed by the relevant Spanish law as the applicable law. However, whilst he had previously been habitually resident in England & Wales, he might well have owned property which became subject to a proprietary estoppel claim. Such a claim would remain subject to the law of England & Wales. The jurisdiction for such claim under the Regulation would however be the courts of Spain, which would apply the relevant Spanish law to all other aspects of the succession but the law of England & Wales to the proprietary estoppel claim provided it was included within the definition of a succession agreement. If the proprietary estoppel claim was based on an oral contract, however the question of its formal validity, which would be outside the scope of the Regulation would be a matter for the Spanish court to resolve without recourse to the Regulation. Subject to such formal validity, other questions as to admissibility and substantive validity and binding effects would be resolved by the Regulation.

The Opening of the Succession

This phrase sounds odd to many practitioners. The start of the process for administration of an estate varies from system to system. The death of the deceased may vest assets directly with executors or heirs, or the succession law may require positive steps to be taken whether intermeddling or some form of acceptance.

Although, art.1.2(c) excludes questions regarding the disappearance or presumed death of a natural person from the scope of the Regulation, a succession may be opened by decisions on such matters.

The order of deaths of more than one person, that are subject to different laws is dealt with below under art. 32.

The Determination of the Beneficiaries and their Respective Shares, the Disposable part of the Estate, the Reserved Shares and other restrictions and Claims of Persons close to the Deceased

As discussed in chapter 2, the nature of inheritance law across different legal systems is extremely varied. "Forced Heirship" is a term often used by common law practitioners to describe civil law inheritance systems. However, all inheritance systems differ markedly.

The inheritance rights of children as against a surviving spouse under the Dutch system are almost non-existent compared to the rights of children under the Napoleonic or Germanic systems. The rights of a surviving cohabitee in England & Wales can be extensive under the Inheritance (Provision for Family and Dependents) Act 1975, whilst non-existent under other systems. The rights of a surviving spouse in France can be very limited whilst under other systems, much more extensive. The legal rights of a surviving spouse under Scottish law may be limited to movable property whilst under Irish law may extend to all of the assets.

Each system will regard itself as different from most others, and a simple common law/civil law division is not usually helpful.

In most civil law systems, the matrimonial property regime must first be dissolved, and then the assets that are within the estate of the deceased can be ascertained. A portion may then be subject to inheritance rights, whilst the remainder will be freely disposable.

Some particular assets such as the family home may be subject to special provisions such as the prior rights of a spouse under Scottish law.

Claims under the Inheritance (Provision for Family and Dependents) Act 1975 in England & Wales can currently only be made if the deceased died domiciled in England and Wales. Although there were Law Commission proposals to amend this restriction, these did not reach the final Inheritance and Trustees' Powers Act 2014.

If the internal succession law of England & Wales is validly chosen under art.22, then *renvoi* is not accepted. Is the limitation within s.1(1) of the 1975 Act to the estates of deceased persons domiciled in England & Wales a matter of *renvoi* or an entry condition? As is argued in chapter 22, it does seem likely that the courts of SR Zone states will not regard themselves as bound by this restriction, regard it as a matter of UK private international law and therefore excluded under art.34. This would seem to be the intention behind the Regulation; that a valid choice of law should bring with it, the whole of that law.

Other jurisdictions have limitations in relation to the *situs* of property. For example, the Succession (Scotland) Act 1964 removed the right of a surviving spouse to a usufruct (the widow's *terce* or the widower's *courtesy*) in one third of heritable (immovable) property on the death of a spouse. Since 1964 Scottish succession legal (as opposed to prior) rights apply only to the movable property of Scottish domiciled persons. Changes to this division have often been suggested but not yet implemented. A valid *professio juris* of Scottish law, is likely to bring with it the obligations of legal rights in relation to worldwide movables even though the deceased may not have died domiciled in Scotland. However, it is presumed that the non-application of Scottish legal rights to immovable property would be respected for the succession as a whole.

Similar arguments apply to estate administration law that is considered in chapter 16.

Capacity to Inherit, Disinheritance and Disqualification by conduct

The legal capacity of natural persons is excluded by art.1.2(b), but other questions such as the status of unborn children or of legal persons not yet created, will be governed by the applicable succession law. The status of minor beneficiaries and acceptance by them is considered in chapter 20.

Questions on disqualification by conduct such as whether the murder of the deceased automatically disqualifies an heir, and whether such disqualification can be adjusted, will be a matter for the applicable law.

The transfer of the assets, rights and obligations making up the estate to the legatees

The administration of a succession is the subject of chapter 16 and the question of debts, chapter 17. Under some legal systems assets vest directly in executors or in heirs. In other systems, assets may only vest on the appointment of administrators or particular heirs. When and how assets vest and whether they must be transferred by an adminstrator or one or more of the heirs will all be governed by the applicable law.

Generally, if there is no valid *professio juris,* then *renvoi* of administration to differing systems will be accepted, whilst if there is a valid *professio juris* then no such *renvoi* is accepted and all administration should be carried out under the relevant internal law.

The extent and obligation to pay debts is also very varied between systems and to the surprise of some can be unlimited and extend beyond the size of the estate. Again these matters will be governed by the applicable succession law and not the local law.

Special Restrictive Rules on Particularly sited assets

Article 30 provides an exception to the general applicable law rule and permits the use of local inheritance rules in relation to "…certain immovable property, certain enterprises or other categories of assets….which for economic, family or social considerations, impose restrictions concerning or affecting the succession.. ".

Some systems, such as the Tyrol in Austria, restrict the inheritance of farms to prevent them being taken over by holiday makers. Para. 112 of the Waters Report suggests that immovables "would refer clearly to such assets as family farms, or interests in family farms less than full proprietorship, where the duration of the interest or the nature and quantum of rights attached to the interest reflect a particular inheritance scheme. 'Special categories of assets' would refer for example to historic articles, such as sculptures, paintings and jewellery within the family which are required by the original act of disposition to pass from generation to generation down the lineal line."

Recital 54 of the Regulation tries to limit art.30 stating that "this exception to the application of the law applicable to the succession requires a strict interpretation in order to remain compatible with the general objective of this Regulation. Therefore, neither conflict-of-laws rules subjecting immovable property to a law different from that applicable to movable property nor provisions providing for a reserved share of the estate greater than that provided for in the law applicable to the succession under this Regulation may be regarded as constituting special rules imposing restrictions concerning or affecting the succession in respect of certain assets."

Commorientes

Article 32 is the only provision in the Regulation that directly amends material succession law as opposed to private international law, but is almost word for word the same as article 13 of HccH32.

If more than one person dies at the same time or if the order of deaths is uncertain and if different laws apply to this question, then the order of deaths might be regarded as different under different laws. This provision overrides the applicable laws so that in effect each person is deemed to have died before the other. Paras. 106 and 107 of the Waters Report sets this out in some detail.

This problem will however occur in any event in relation to questions of presumption of death, since this is excluded from the scope of the Regulation under art.1.2(c).

Bona Vacantia

Article 33 is concerned, as described in para. 114 of the Waters Report "with the right of the State to take for itself those assets in the estate of the deceased to which there is no testate or intestate heir. Two positions exist as to the nature of these rights. States following the theory of the regalian right, take the view that, when there is no designated beneficiary under a will and no physical heir to take on intestacy, the State takes as *bona vacantia* all estate assets whose situs is in that State. States of the civil law tradition are divided; some adopt the contrary position that the State takes as an heir (the *ultimus heres)* in those circumstances where there is no testamentary beneficiary and no physical heir. ... these two positions can lead to both positive conflicts and negative conflicts. A positive conflict occurs when the State upholding *situs* and the State upholding *ultimus heres* both claim to be entitled; a negative conflict will exist when State X *(ultimus heres)* is the situs of the assets, but X designates State Y (the regalian right) as the ultimate heir. So neither claims entitlement."

Article 33 protects the right of the State with *situs* to claim assets which under the applicable law would pass to another state. However, the rights are more limited than under the equivalent provision, article 16 of HccH32. Article 33 only applies if there is no heir or legatee for any assets under a DoPuD and will therefore not apply to a partial intestacy. In addition as stated in recital 56 to the Regulation, the proviso enables creditors to seek satisfaction of their claims out of all the assets of the estate, irrespective of their location.

Other Aspects of Chapter III

Other particular aspects of Chapter III also merit discussion in individual chapters. Most importantly chapter 21 deals with art.22 and the *professio juris.* Articles 24 – 27 on DoPuDs are considered in chapter 15, art.28 dealing with acceptance or waiver in in chapter 17, art.29 in relation to administrators in chapter 16, art. 31 dealing with rights *in rem* in chapter 19, art.34 on *renvoi* in chapter 22, art.35 on public policy in chapter 24 and arts.36 – 38 on multi-system states in chapter 21.

CHAPTER EIGHT

GENERAL PROVISIONS – CHAPTER VII OF THE REGULATION

This part of the Regulation contains various mopping up provisions.

Article 75 dealing with existing international treaties is looked at in detail in chapter 23 of this book, whilst arts.80 and 81 establishing the comitology, committee and forms is considered in chapter 12. The very important transitional provisions of art. 83 are dealt with in chapter 21.

Some have argued that the transitional provisions of art.83.4 considered in detail in chapter 21 can only apply to DoPuDs made after 17 August 2012, but there is no authority to support such an interpretation.

Article 76 makes it clear that the Insolvency Regulation[82] can still apply even if the debtor has died. Different member states have differing rules, and the Insolvency Regulation takes precedence in relation to matters of jurisdiction and applicable law ahead of the Regulation.

Articles 77 – 79 requires member states to:

- Make certain information available to the public within the framework of the European Judicial Network, and keep and update fact sheets regarding the registration of immovable property; and

[82] (EC) No. 1346/2000 of 29 May 2000

- Give details of courts, authorities and procedures to the Commission, to enable the Commission to publish a list of such authorities.

https://beta.e-justice.europa.eu/380/EN/succession?clang=en enables a search to be made as to the relevant courts and authorities in each member state. However, as decided by the CJEU in the case of *W.B.*[83] the list is not definitive.

Article 82 requires the Commission to submit a reviewing report to the Parliament and the Council together with proposals for amendment to the Regulation by 18 August 2025.

Article 84 brought the Regulation into force on 17 August 2012. The Regulation applied from 17 August 2015, although arts.77 and 78 (on public information) applied from 16 January 2014 and arts, 79, 80 and 81 (the list to be prepared by the Commission and comitology) from 5 July 2012.

The final provision of article 84 states that "This Regulation shall be binding in its entirety and directly applicable in the Member States in accordance with the Treaties." The Treaty on the Functioning of the European Union indicates that a third country is one that is not a Member State[84] whilst the expression Member State includes all Member States that are parties to the EU Treaties. There is no specific definition of 'Member State' or 'third State' in the Regulation.

In older EU Regulations, such a definition is included, restricting the definition of a Member State to those that are bound by the specific Regulation. There was some academic debate as to whether the definition of Member State should or should not include those Member States,

---

83 C-658/17

84 See for example article 63 of the TFEU.

Denmark and Ireland (and previously the United Kingdom) not bound by the Regulation.

Recitals 82 and 83 make it clear that Denmark and Ireland (and the United Kingdom) are not bound by or subject to the application of the Regulation. It is now generally accepted that CJEU would agree with the EU Institutions that Denmark and Ireland are therefore not included within the definition of a Member State for the purposes of the Regulation.

CHAPTER NINE

JURISDICTION – CHAPTER II OF THE REGULATION

Since many private client practitioners are not litigators, matters of jurisdiction are usually not high up our list of priorities. However, the creation by the Regulation of one court with universal jurisdiction throughout the European Union, is perhaps the provision with the most far reaching of effects. Court decisions in the SR Zone are now recognised and fully enforceable across the zone.

The law of the forum having jurisdiction is important, not only, as the starting point for determining the relevant connecting factor for the applicable succession law and whether any *professio juris* is valid, but also for the process of determining other incidental questions such as:

- the matrimonial regime of a spouse
- whether an asset is a movable or an immovable
- the status of a beneficiary as married or divorced, adopted or legitimated
- whether or not joint or other property structures such as trusts pass outside the estate

Any estate planning should begin by considering whether a Member State is likely to have universal jurisdiction, whether this is what is wanted and whether it can be changed.

The exercise by the testator of a valid *professio juris* not only may change the applicable succession law but does then also enable the "parties concerned" to elect for that state of nationality to take jurisdiction, provided that it is a Member State. This option, may be very important for some families.

Universal Jurisdiction in an EU Member State under Article 4

Under art.4 of the Regulation, the courts of the Member State in which the deceased had his habitual residence at the time of death, have jurisdiction to rule on the succession as a whole. If someone dies habitually resident in a Member State, there is no way to avoid a Member State having universal jurisdiction in relation to all assets worldwide.

The definition of a "Court" includes notaries and other legal professionals, if they are exercising a judicial function. As a result, if a court or a notary is not exercising a judicial function, then they are outside the scope of the Regulation. This view is supported by CJEU. [85]

Jurisdiction under art.4 applies to all court "Decisions" as defined by art.3.1(g) including a determination of costs provided that they relate to a matter of succession as defined by art.3.1(a).

The universal nature of the jurisdiction relating to the succession as a whole, attached to a last habitual residence in the European Union, has been widely criticised as overly imperialistic since it may well conflict with the jurisdiction of third States under their different private international connecting factors such as nationality or domicile.[86] The practical limits of this universal jurisdiction are considered below.

---

85 Article 3.2 and Recitals 20 and 21 and see the cases of *WB* C-658/17, *E.E* C-80/19 and *Albausy* C-187/23.

86 See for example *Le droit européen des successions* by Bonomi and Wautelet 2nd Edition p.188 onwards

Oberle

The judgment of the CJEU in *Oberle* C-20/17 was published on 21 June 2018.

CJEU decisions coming from a civil law tradition have to be unanimous and are therefore always concise. What is not stated is often as important as what is. The Opinion of the Advocate General (AG) Szpunar, who was also the Advocate General in the case of *Mahnkopf*, was published in February 2018 and is very helpful.

Adrien Théodore (Adrien) Oberle, a French national, who had his last habitual residence in France, died on 28 November 2015. Adrien left behind two sons, one of whom, Vincent Pierre (Vincent) Oberle, was the appellant in the proceedings. The assets of the estate were located in France and Germany. Vincent subsequently applied to the German court Amtsgericht Schöneberg (in Berlin) — as the court having jurisdiction under German law relating to the succession of non-residents — for the issuing of a national certificate of succession limited to the estate located in Germany. That certificate was to state that the estate was inherited by Vincent and his brother under French law.

However, the Amtsgericht Schöneberg declared that it lacked jurisdiction to issue a national certificate of succession because the national law must yield to the provisions of the EUSR. This meant that the French courts, as the courts of the Member State where the deceased had his habitual residence at the time of death, and not the German courts, had jurisdiction to rule on the succession as a whole, including on Vincent's application. Vincent contested that decision which was then referred to the CJEU.

The Advocate General's opinion sets out that national certificates are not outside the scope of the Regulation and carefully considered the interplay of art. 4 dealing with jurisdiction and art. 62(3) relating to the European Certificate of Succession (ECS – see chapter 12) which states:

> "3. The Certificate shall not take the place of internal documents used for similar purposes in the Member States. ..."

Chapter VI of the Regulation dealing with the ECS is perhaps not the best drafted part of the Regulation and art. 62(2) stating "2. The use of the Certificate shall not be mandatory" is somewhat confusing.

The German Government argued that an interpretation of art.4 of the Regulation leading to its application in relation to procedures for issuing national certificates of succession would mean that the use of the ECS would be mandatory in practice.

However, the Advocate General considered that art. 4 of the Regulation does not stop the issuing of national certificates of succession in the Member State with jurisdiction. He also argued that art. 62(3) and not art.62(2) solely deals with the relationship between the ECS and national certificates of succession. Article 62(2) relates not only to national certificates of succession, but also — as is clear from the guidance set out in the second sentence of recital 69 thereof — to all 'instruments available under [the] Regulation' which heirs are free to use. Therefore, the Advocate General did not consider that the determination of jurisdiction over procedures for issuing national certificates of succession under art. 4 of the Regulation meant that the use of the ECS was mandatory in practice.

The conclusion of the Advocate General and the decision of the CJEU that jurisdiction under art. 4 on the basis of the last habitual residence also includes questions as to national certificates, is not surprising bearing in mind the purpose of the Regulation. The Polish Government and the EU Commission supported this view. It was interesting that the German, French and Portuguese Governments opposed this view and that the referral to the CJEU was necessary in the first place. Member States are still having difficulty in coming to terms with the wide-ranging effects of the Regulation.

The opinion of the AG covers numbers of interesting issues, including consideration of the definitions of "court" and "decision" under art.3 and at Footnote 27 reference to the various succession treaties that still override the Regulation considered later in chapter 23.

Changing Universal Jurisdiction to another EU Member State under Articles 5, 6 and 7

Provided that the deceased exercised a choice of law option in favour of another Member State, then under art.7 there are three mechanisms for jurisdiction to be taken by the courts of the Member State so chosen.

The first is if the courts with universal jurisdiction under art.4 have declined jurisdiction, under art.6(a), which they may do at the request of one of the parties.

The second is if under art.5, the "parties concerned" have agreed that the other Member State shall have jurisdiction. It is probable that reference to the "parties concerned" refers solely to beneficiaries or heirs and does not include creditors.[87] Some testators may therefore exercise a valid *professio juris* solely for the purposes of enabling their family heirs to move jurisdiction (and all administration) back to their home Member State after the testator's death, rather than for any differences of the applicable succession law. Article 5.2 sets out that the choice must be exercised by the parties concerned in writing, dated and signed by them. If such a choice is made by all the parties, then any court with universal jurisdiction under art.4 must under art.6(b) decline jurisdiction.

The third mechanism is if all the parties to the proceeedings have expressly accepted the jurisdiction of the court seised.

---

87 See also the case of *Saponaro* C-565/16.

In the case of *RK*[88], the deceased had made a German language Will in 1990, and by virtue of art.83.4, this was deemed to be a *professio juris* of German law under art.22.

CJEU decided that arts.6(a) and 7(a) must be interpreted as meaning that the rules of jurisdiction set out in those provisions also apply in the event that, in his or her will, drawn up before 17 August 2015, the deceased had not chosen the law applicable to the succession, but the designation of that law is deemed solely by art. 83(4).

The deceased died habitually resident in Spain.

The other point at issue was whether or not the Spanish court with universal jurisdiction had actually declined jurisdiction under art.6(a).

By order of 29 April 2019, the Juzgado de Primera Instancia e Instrucción n.º 3 de Estepona (Court of First Instance and Preliminary Investigations No 3, Estepona, Spain), before which CR had brought an action, decided to 'refrain from hearing or determining [the succession proceedings before that court], on the ground that the German courts [were] better placed to rule on the succession and on account of the practical circumstances, such as the habitual residence of the party concerned in [that] matter and the location of the essential part of the estate'.

This is an example of linguistic difficulty. The Spanish Government pointed out in its written observations, that there is a difference in the wordings of arts.6(a) and 7(a) in the Spanish-language version, by contrast with the other language versions.

In the Spanish-language version, art. 6(a) uses the expression '*abstenerse de conocer*', and art. 7(a) of uses the verb '*inhibirse*'. By contrast, other language versions use terms which expressly refer to declining jurisdiction. Thus, for example, the German-language version uses '*für*

[88] C-422/20

unzuständig erklären', the English-language version uses '*decline jurisdiction*', the French-language version uses '*décliner sa compétence*', the Italian-language version uses '*dichiarare la propria incompetenza*' and the Romanian-language version uses '*decline competența*'.

In this case, the Spanish court used the terms of the Spanish-language version of art. 6(a) when stating that it 'refrains from hearing and determining the present proceedings'.

The CJEU found that in order for there to have been a declining of jurisdiction, within the meaning of art. 6(a), in favour of the courts of the Member State whose law was chosen by the deceased, it is not necessary for the court previously seised to have expressly declined jurisdiction, but that intention must be unequivocally apparent from the decision that it delivered in that regard.

CJEU also declared that arts.6(a), 7(a) and 39 must be interpreted as meaning that the court of the Member State seised following a declining of jurisdiction is not competent to examine whether the conditions set out in those provisions were satisfied in order for the court previously seised to decline jurisdiction.

Universal Jurisdiction in an EU Member State under Article 10

If the habitual residence of the deceased was not in a Member State, art.10 sets out a hierarchy of subsidiary jurisdictions:

(a) the courts of a Member State in which there are assets of the deceased, will have jurisdiction to rule on the succession as a whole if either the deceased had:

i. The nationality of that Member State at the time of death or if not

ii. His previous habitual residence had been in that Member State within the last five years or if not

(b) the courts of the Member State with assets situated there shall have jurisdiction in relation to those assets.

There is no tie breaker provision if the deceased had multiple nationalities or multiple previous residences.

Therefore, if someone dies resident in a third State, generally Member States will only have jurisdiction limited to the assets in that own state. However, under Art. 10, if the deceased has assets at death in a Member State of which they were a national or in which they had been habitually resident in the previous 5 years, that Member State will have universal jurisdiction. This latter has become known as the "piano" jurisdiction, since there is no *de minimis* limit. If a French national dies with a piano in France, but nothing else, in theory, France will have universal worldwide jurisdiction even though the deceased died habitually resident outside the European Union. Getting assets out of such jurisdictions may be important for some citizens. Piano removal firms may now be doing better business.

In in the case of *VA and ZA v TP*,[89] XA, a French national, died in September 2015 in France and the succession was opened in France. It was subsequently decided by the Versailles court of appeal, that XA was at the time of his death still habitually resident in England.

The CJEU by implication confirmed that the United Kingdom was not a Member State under the Regulation and confirmed that a court of a Member State must raise of its own motion its jurisdiction under the rule of subsidiary jurisdiction under art.10.1 where, having first been seised on the basis of the rule of general jurisdiction under art. 4, it subsequently finds that it has no jurisdiction under that article.

[89] C-645/20

The matter was remitted back to France and decided in the Cour de Cassation.[90] Given XA's French nationality and his ownership of assets in France as at the date of his death, the Cour de Cassation found that French courts had jurisdiction to rule on his succession as a whole under art. 10.1. By failing to raise of its own motion its jurisdiction under the subsidiary jurisdiction rule, when, having been seised on the basis art.4, it found it had no jurisdiction under that article, the Versailles court of appeal was in violation of art. 10.1.

The case of *Jurtukala*[91] makes it clear that subsidiary jurisdiction under art. 10.1(a) may only be used if there is no principal jurisdiction in a Member State within the SR Zone under art. 4.

BF, a Polish national died in Hamburg, Germany, leaving immovable property in Poland. The district court in Poland declined jurisdiction on the basis that the court in Hamburg had jurisdiction under art. 4. A superior Polish court held that the district court did have supplementary jurisdiction. CJEU disagreed and made it clear that the rule of subsidiary jurisdiction laid down by art. 10 applies only where the habitual residence of the deceased at the time of death was located in a Member State not bound by the Regulation or in a third State.

Limitation of proceedings under Article 12

It is however the limitations on universal jurisdiction contained in article 12 that are perhaps the most relevant for practitioners in third states.

> *1. Where the estate of the deceased comprises assets located in a third State, the court seised to rule on the succession may, at the request of one of the parties, decide not to rule on one or more of such assets if it may be expected that its decision in respect of those assets will not be*

[90] Cour de Cassation 21 September 2022 pourvoi no 19-15.438

[91] C-55/23

recognised and, where applicable, declared enforceable in that third State.

2. Paragraph 1 shall not affect the right of the parties to limit the scope of the proceedings under the law of the Member State of the court seised.

This is a somewhat strange provision, which has no similar model in any other EU regulation and is not referred to in the Recitals to the Regulation. It does not really limit jurisdiction but gives the court discretion not to rule on particular assets in third States. This could be seen as superfluous since recognition and enforcement will be governed locally by such third States in any event.

Many legal systems in the EU do not permit courts to exercise discretion, and this article may sit uncomfortably in such systems. The article can only be invoked at the request of one of the parties and only in relation to the assets specified by that party. If invoked, it is unclear as to the matters which the court should take into account when considering whether to exercise its discretion and exclude itself from ruling on particular assets.

It might well be that if the court has universal jurisdiction by virtue of article 10, the deceased dying habitually resident in a third State with limited assets in the state of universal jurisdiction, then it may be more inclined to agree to limit its ruling under article 12. However, if the deceased exercised a valid *professio juris* in favour of the law of the state of nationality within the EU, so that *renvoi* applicable in third States would not be permitted under art. 34 (see chapter 22), then it might be expected that the court with universal jurisdiction would refuse to exclude assets in a third State.

There will be harder cases in between these two extremes. Whether assets are subject to claw back under the applicable law but not in the third State might also be a relevant factor and in due course no doubt the CJEU will consider the provisions of the article.

No Universal Jurisdiction in an EU Member State

If the deceased was not a national of a Member State with assets in it and had not had a previous habitual residence in such a state within five years before death, then each Member State with assets in it, has jurisdiction limited to those assets only. Multiple jurisdictions will therefore continue to apply in such cases if there are assets in more than one EU Member State.

There are other provisions including a *Forum Necessitatis* in art.11 and for *Lis Pendens* in art.17 with which practitioners within the European Union will need to be familiar.

Specific Jurisdiction in relation to Waivers

Under art.13 the courts of a Member State in which a person declaring an acceptance or waiver, is habitually resident, have jurisdiction in relation to such acceptance or waiver as demonstrated in the case of *TN and NN v* EG[92]. The subsequent case of *Ławida*[93] made it clear that such subsidiary jurisdiction is limited solely to taking the acceptance or waiver. Both cases are dealt with later in chapter 15.

Injunctions, Anti-Suit Injunctions and Anti-Anti-Suit Injunctions

In some cases, the courts will grant an injunction in order to restrain foreign proceedings; an anti-suit injunction.

In *Morris v Davies*[94] the deceased was a British citizen thought to be domiciled in England & Wales but who died in 2008 in Paris and habitually resident in France or Belgium. The executor under an English

---

[92] C-617/20

[93] C-57/24

[94] [2011] EWHC 1272 (Ch)

will sought an anti-suit injunction against family members in order to prevent them claiming in Belgium. The court referred to the Court of Appeal decision in *Seismic Shipping v Total E&P*[95], that "the existence of two parallel sets of proceedings is a weighty factor when determining whether to exercise the discretion to grant an injunction, but is not in itself enough to justify such an order. It is necessary also to consider whether the ends of justice require an injunction to be granted and that two conditions are satisfied namely that the English court is the natural forum for the resolution of the dispute and that the conduct of the defendants is vexatious, oppressive or unconscionable."

The decision in *Turner v Grovit*[96] found that the grant of anti-suit relief is precluded if an action fell within the scope of the Brussels I Regulation.

The question as to whether any decision of the Belgian court would be recognised in England or vice versa and the applicability or otherwise of the 1934 Treaty between the UK and Belgium do not appear to have been considered in Morris v Davies. If a decision would not be recognised in either direction, it is difficult to see that the ends of justice require an injunction. Although the UK has never been bound by the Regulation, it has been part of the EU *acquis* and the law of the UK from 2012 until 2021. With due respect, it would appear contrary to general provisions of comity, if a court would now agree to grant an anti-suit injunction in relation to proceedings in a Member State that had universal jurisdiction under the Regulation, particularly if in any state other than Belgium with which the UK has the 1934 Treaty, in which such a decision would not be recognised or enforceable in the UK in any event.

95 [2005] Lloyds Reports 359

96 [2004] WL 5400365

As in an arms race, other jurisdictions may counter by ordering an anti-anti-suit injunction and courts in the EU are now beginning to do so.[97] We have not yet had an anti-anti-anti-suit injunction.

What is perhaps more interesting is whether parties could be required to request the court in the SR Zone to limit proceedings under art.12, so that any decision would not infringe the jurisdiction of the court concerned.

97 As in the case of 21 O 9512/19 Regional Court Munich I http://eplaw.org/wp-content/uploads/2019/12/DE-AASI-HRC-Munich-6-U-5042-19-EN.pdf

CHAPTER TEN

RECOGNITION AND ENFORCEMENT – CHAPTER IV OF THE REGULATION

This book is written for practitioners outside the EU SR Zone. Accordingly, Chapter IV of the Regulation on the recognition and enforcement of decisions between the Member States bound by the Regulation, is of limited relevance. However, the creation by the Regulation of one court with universal jurisdiction throughout the European Union, is perhaps the provision with the most far reaching of effects. Court decisions in the SR Zone are now recognised and fully enforceable across the zone. Authentic instruments are also accepted and enforced as described in the next chapter.

Articles 39 to 58 set out in detail the mechanics in this changed landscape for the recognition and enforcement of Decisions, as defined in art.3.1(g).

The definition of Decisions, does include both contentious and non-contentious court decisions, but they must be from the Court of a Member State. Thus, decisions from third States will not be recognised and enforced within the SR Zone, under the Regulation, but under each Member State's system outside the scope of the Regulation. Whether decisions from courts within the SR Zone are recognised and enforced in third States is of course a matter for the individual legal systems of those third States.

For the UK, the existence of the 1934 treaty with Belgium, considered in chapter 23 should not be overlooked. The treaties between Member States and other third States are also considered in that chapter.

Court, as defined in art.3.2 does include, not only judicial authorities, but also all other authorities and legal professionals with legal competence in succession matters:

- exercising a judicial function, or
- acting by delegation of power by a judicial authority, or
- acting under the control of a judicial authority.

The question as to whether a notary might be acting as a court was considered in the cases of *W.B.*[98] and *E.E.*[99] and the consequences of non-notification by Member States of which legal professionals are within this definition, are considered in the next chapter, chapter 11.

Interestingly in the case of *Albausy*[100] the CJEU held that the German court was not exercising a judicial function when issuing a European Certificate of Succession under art. 67, and therefore had no standing to bring questions to the CJEU.

A Decision should be differentiated from a Court Settlement as defined in art.3.2(h). Authentic Instrument also has a separate definition under art.3.2(i). The acceptance of Authentic Instruments and the enforceability of them and of Court Settlements is dealt with in Chapter V of the Regulation also dealt with in the next chapter.

Further details of the provisions of Chapter IV of the Regulation are not considered and readers who need to, should consult other sources.

---

98 C-658/17

99 C-80/19

100 C-187/23

CHAPTER ELEVEN

COURTS, COURT SETTLEMENTS, AUTHENTIC INSTRUMENTS AND NOTARIES – CHAPTER V OF THE REGULATION

Chapter V of the Regulation deals with documents, such as authentic instruments and court settlements, that affect the administration of a succession, outside court decisions that are separately recognised and enforced as considered in the previous chapter.

Courts, Rulings, Decisions and Settlements

The relevant definitions are somewhat circular.

The CJEU has decided that in order to determine whether a body making a reference is a court for the purposes of TFEU, "the Court takes account of a number of factors, such as whether the body is established by law, whether it is permanent, whether its jurisdiction is compulsory, whether its procedure is *inter partes*, whether it applies rules of law and whether it is independent."[101] Article 3.2 of the Regulation extends this definition of Court to include non-judicial authorities if exercising a judicial authority.

Decisions are very broadly defined in art.3.1(g) as "any decision in a matter of succession given by a court of a Member State, whatever the decision may be called, including a decision on the determination of costs

[101] C-54/96 at para. 23

or expenses by an office of the court". A Decision is a decision…Some definitions are more helpful than others.

The meaning of decision in art.3.1(g) has not been considered directly by the CJEU. However, in the case of *Oberle,*[102] the question was considered obliquely but in some detail by the AG. That case revolved around the question as to whether courts in a cross-border case other than those with jurisdiction under art.4 could deal with local succession certificates.

The German and Polish Governments and the Commission referred to a certain peculiarity of art. 4 of the German language version of the Regulation, which refers to the courts of the Member States having jurisdiction 'for decisions on matters of succession' ('*für Entscheidungen in Erbsachen*').

The wording of the German version of the Regulation could be an indication that this provision determines jurisdiction only over procedures in which the courts of the Member States give a 'decision' for the purpose of art.3.1(g). However, in other language versions of the Regulation, the term 'deciding' does not occur in art. 4; instead those versions refer to the concept of 'ruling' on the succession. Therefore, the German language wording of the Regulation cannot be regarded as decisive.

The distinction between the use of the verb "to rule" in art.4 as opposed to "decision" in other parts of the Regulation, indicates that art. 4 jurisdiction is given to a court both for judicial and non-judicial authority. Similarly, recitals 20, 21, 22 and 36 make it clear that 'non-judicial authorities' which do not exercise judicial functions are not bound by the rules of jurisdiction under the Regulation. There is no reference to 'judicial authorities', which are therefore presumed to be bound by the rules of jurisdiction even when acting non-judicially.

---

102 C-20/17

The AG noted the difficulty in establishing what meaning should be attached to the term 'rule'. Article 3.1(g) only defines 'decision', and that it was not obvious that reference to 'ruling' by the courts, in fact was identical to the term 'decision' as defined under art.3.1(g). These difficulties are all the greater when most language versions of the Regulation use the same word 'decision' in art. 3.1(g) in order to define the term 'decision' (*idem per idem*).

Similarly, a Court settlement is defined in art. 3.1(h) as "a settlement in a matter of succession which has been approved by a court or concluded before a court in the course of proceedings".

Notaries, Courts and Authentic Instruments

Authentic Instrument also has a separate definition under art.3.1(i), being "a document in a matter of succession which has been formally drawn up or registered as an authentic instrument in a Member State and the authenticity of which:

i. relates to the signature and the content of the authentic instrument; and

ii. has been established by a public authority or other authority empowered for that purpose by the Member State of origin."

This definition is again somewhat circular but is modelled on the similar provision in the Brussels I*bis* Regulation. The CJEU 1999 decision in *Unibank*[103] is usually cited as authority for that definition, but that case found that a particular document was not an authentic instrument and did not actually define what such an instrument might be.

[103] C-260/97

Court, as defined in art.3.2 does include, not only judicial authorities, but also all other authorities and legal professionals with legal competence in succession matters:

- exercising a judicial function, or
- acting by delegation of power by a judicial authority, or
- acting under the control of a judicial authority.

A Decision must therefore be differentiated both from a Court Settlement and also an Authentic Instrument. Although it is not specifically stated, recitals 59 and 60 indicate that the definitions of Decision and Authentic Instrument are mutually exclusive. An authentic instrument is not a decision and vice versa. However, this question was put to the CJEU in the case of *W.B.*,[104] but not answered.

The question as to whether a notary might be acting as a court was considered in the cases of *W.B.* and *E.E.*[105] and *OKR.*[106]

W.B.

The decision in *W.B.* dealt with two issues but concerned the question as to whether and in what circumstances, notaries in Poland were to be regarded as a 'court' for the purposes of the Regulation.

Article 3.2 requires EU Member States to notify the European Commission as to the identity of professionals who would be a 'court', but Poland had not done so. WB was a Polish national resident in Poland with a bank account in Germany. The Polish notary issued a certificate

---

[104] C-658/17

[105] C-80/19

[106] C-387/20

of succession, which he believed to be a 'court' decision, but a European certificate of succession could not be issued because Poland had not given notification as to the position of Polish notaries to the Commission.

The CJEU found otherwise. First, it decided that the non-notification by the Polish government was of indicative value only, and that Polish notaries could still be a 'court'.

Although it had already decided that a Polish notary could be a 'court', the CJEU then, however, found that those notarial activities relating to the issuing of a deed of certification of succession may be exercised at the unanimous request of the interested parties, without affecting the prerogatives of the court in the absence of agreement between the parties. This is even though notaries have an obligation, under Polish law, to verify that the legal requirements for issuing a deed of certification of succession are complied with, since they have no decision-making powers.

As a result, notaries preparing such certificates of succession with the agreement of the parties are, as set out in recital 21, not bound by the Regulation rules of jurisdiction, but the certificates, as authentic instruments under Chapter V of the Regulation, should still circulate freely and be accepted throughout the EU.

E.E.

This case related to the succession of a Lithuanian national who died in Germany where she was habitual resident. She was survived by her German spouse and her Lithuanian son to whom she left everything under a notarial will executed in 2013 in Lithuania where her assets were located.

The son requested a notary in Lithuania to issue the relevant Certificate of Succession and generally deal with the succession, whilst under the terms of a declaration signed in Germany the surviving spouse renounced all inheritance and "consented to the jurisdiction of Lithuania." The request was rejected by the notary on the grounds that the deceased's habitual residence was in Germany.

The CJEU in its decision followed the opinion of the Advocate General and confirmed that a civil law notary is not a "court" within the meaning of art. 3.2 unless exercising a judicial function or acting under the delegated power or under the supervision of a judicial authority. Indeed, notaries have no judicial authority if they have no authority to rule or arbitrate on a matter disputed between the parties concerned, such as the deceased's habitual residence, which question then falls within the remit of the courts of justice. Such notaries are therefore not subject to the rules of general jurisdiction of art. 4.

The CJEU confirmed that the definition of the notary's possible judicial authority remained a domestic issue and sent the matter back to Lithuania by reference to arts.4, 5, 22, 83.2 and 83.4.

OKR

OKR asked a Polish notary to draw up a notarial will containing a clause stipulating that the law applicable to the succession at issue in the main proceedings would be Ukrainian law. The notary refused, on the basis of arts.22 and 75 of the Regulation and the Treaty between Poland and Ukraine of 24 May 1993.

OKR brought a complaint, against the refusal to perform the requested notarial act before the Regional Court, Opole, Poland, pursuant to Article 83 § 1 of the Polish Law on Notaries.

The CJEU in its decision again followed the opinion of the Advocate General and confirmed that since a civil law notary is not a "court" within the meaning of art.3.2 (unless exercising a judicial function or acting under the delegated power or under the supervision of a judicial authority) and therefore no standing to bring a matter to CJEU.

The facts of the case came back to CJEU in the case of *OP*[107] which is considered later in relation to Treaties with third States in chapter 23.

NJ[108]

This CJEU case concerned the rights of the employees of a Spanish notarial practice the ownership of which was transferred. The fact that the Spanish Government had registered notaries as courts for the purposes of the Succession Regulation and for the issuing of an ECS, did not take them outside the rules protecting employees.

Enforceability

Articles 60 and 61 deal with the enforceability of authentic instruments and court settlements (i.e. not court decisions). Whilst the evidentiary effects of authentic instruments are referred to in art.59, the material effects of both authentic instruments and court settlements is not covered. It may be that they only have the enforceable effects that they would have in the Member State of Enforcement.

And?

Where does this leave us?

Although there may be some disagreement, it would seem for the moment that it will be rare for a notary to be acting as a court. Under many systems it is notaries who produce the European Certificate of Succession (ECS, described in the next chapter). An ECS having its own

---

107 C-21/22

108 C-583/21 (and 584 – 586/21)

effects, is different to an authentic instrument. The ECS can only be issued in the Member State whose courts have jurisdiction.

Therefore, although notaries are not subject to the jurisdictional limits of art.4, they are so limited in relation to an ECS. They are therefore limited to producing local certificates of succession and other authentic instruments, which can all circulate freely. However, their effects will be those under the law where they are made, whilst the effects of an ECS are set out in art.69. In a cross-border succession, it may well be that an ECS from the Member State with jurisdiction, may generally be preferred to an authentic instrument from a different state.

Some notaries might well have preferred if they were to be regarded as a "court". If non-notification under art. 3.2 is not conclusive, notification may also be non-conclusive. The development of notaries acting outside the scope of the Regulation (and other regulations such as Brussels II *ter*), has been called dejurisdictionalisation. Such notarial acts can cause issues such as limping marriages and divorces which may not be recognised in another jurisdiction. Limping succession documents are also best avoided. Developments in this area are very likely. Like it or not, authentic instruments are within the scope of the Regulation and the thrust of the decision in *Oberle*[109] points to notaries even when not acting as courts being be brought within the ambit of art.64. To do otherwise would undermine the purpose of the Regulation.This may well be a subject that is considered further when the Regulation is reviewed in 2025.

[109] C-20/17

CHAPTER TWELVE

FORMS AND COMITOLOGY AND THE EUROPEAN CERTIFICATE OF SUCCESSION – CHAPTER VI OF THE REGULATION

Comitology was a European Union term for the way in which law is modified or adjusted and was somewhat controversial, since comitology was created through committees over which the European Parliament had no oversight. The system was overhauled under the Lisbon Treaty and article 290 TFEU introduced the ability for regulations and directives to contain delegated acts which may delegate to the Commission the power subject to conditions to adopt non-legislative acts of general application to supplement or amend certain non-essential elements of the regulation or directive.

Regulation (EU) 182/2011[110] lays down the rules and general principles concerning mechanisms for control by Member States of the Commission's exercise of implementing powers. Article 80 of the Succession Regulation set out the power for delegated acts in relation to various forms and art. 81 created a comitology committee.

The various forms for use on matters within the scope of the Succession Regulation were created by regulation (EU) No 1329/2014 of 9 December 2014[111] which in article 1 sets out that:

---

110 https://eur-lex.europa.eu/legal-content/en/ALL/?uri=CELEX:32011R0182

111 https://eur-lex.europa.eu/legal-content/EN/TXT/?uri=uriserv:OJ.L.2014.359.01.0030.01.ENG

1. The form to be used for the attestation concerning a decision in a matter of succession referred to in Article 46(3)(b) of Regulation (EU) No 650/2012 shall be as set out in Annex 1 as Form I.

2. The form to be used for the attestation concerning an authentic instrument in a matter of succession referred to in Articles 59(1) and 60(2) of Regulation (EU) No 650/2012 shall be as set out in Annex 2 as Form II.

3. The form to be used for the attestation concerning a court settlement in a matter of succession referred to in Article 61(2) of Regulation (EU) No 650/2012 shall be as set out in Annex 3 as Form III.

4. The form to be used for the application for a European Certificate of Succession referred to in Article 65(2) of Regulation (EU) No 650/2012 shall be as set out in Annex 4 as Form IV.

5. The form to be used for the European Certificate of Succession referred to in Article 67(1) of Regulation (EU) No 650/2012 shall be as set out in Annex 5 as Form V.

During 2019, the CJEU decided the matter of *Brisch*[112] and found that for the purposes of the Regulation it is not compulsory to use the Form IV in Annex 4 to regulation (EU) No 1329/2014, but that it is optional. It was puzzling as to why this case had been brought, but under German law, notaries must read out the whole of documents that they legalise and many of them find it difficult to read out a document set out as a form and therefore often prefer to set matters out in a more readable style.

It is presumed that the use of the other three forms will also be optional, although in practice, "courts" will normally use Forms I and III.

---

[112] C-102/18

It is difficult to see a European Certificate of Succession (ECS) being issued other than in Form V.[113]

In practice non-EU practitioners, are unlikely generally to see or use any of the first four forms, since it is only in member states bound by the Regulation that the forms are available and effective. However, the forms do repay some study. In addition, the ECS set out as Form V can be of particular relevance.

Articles 62–73 in Chapter VI of the Regulation make provision for the validity and effects of the ECS. It is intended to provide proof of the capacity of the heir or legatee and of the powers of executors of wills and administrators of the estate (art.63).

The concept of the EU grant of representation that could be used across borders in the EU, was politically very attractive. However, it is clear that it is only authorities within a member state bound by the Regulation that can issue an ECS.

Local succession certificates can still be issued, art.62.2 stating that, "the use of the European Certificate of Succession shall not be mandatory." In addition, art.62.3 states that, "the certificate shall not be a substitute for internal documents used for similar purposes in the Member States."

Recitals 67 to 72 do clarify the meaning of these provisions. Persons entitled are to be under no obligation to use the ECS, but are free to use the other instruments available under the Regulation.

The judgment of the CJEU in *Oberle*[114] is relevant to these questions.

Adrien Théodore (Adrien) Oberle, a French national, who had his last habitual residence in France, died on 28 November 2015. Adrien left

---

[113] Case C-301/20 will decide whether an ECS without an expiry date is valid.

[114] C-20/17

behind two sons, one of whom, Vincent Pierre (Vincent) Oberle, was the appellant in the proceedings. The assets of the estate were located in France and Germany. Vincent subsequently applied to the German court Amtsgericht Schöneberg (in Berlin) – as the court having jurisdiction under German law relating to the succession of non-residents – for the issuing of a national certificate of succession limited to the estate located in Germany. That certificate was to state that the estate was inherited by Vincent and his brother under French law.

However, the Amtsgericht Schöneberg declared that it lacked jurisdiction to issue a national certificate of succession because the national law must yield to the provisions of the Regulation. This meant that the French courts, as the courts of the Member State where the deceased had his habitual residence at the time of death, and not the German courts, had jurisdiction to rule on the succession as a whole, including on Vincent's application. Vincent contested that decision which was then referred to the CJEU.

The opinion of Advocate General Szpunar set out that national certificates are not outside the scope of the Regulation and carefully considered the interplay of art.4 dealing with jurisdiction and art. 62(3) referred to above. The German Government argued that an interpretation of art.4 of the Regulation leading to its application in relation to procedures for issuing national certificates of succession would mean that the use of the ECS would be mandatory in practice.

However, Advocate General Szpunar considered that art. 4 of the Regulation does not stop the issuing of national certificates of succession in the Member State with jurisdiction, but does do so in other Member States. He also argued that art. 62.3 alone and not art.62.2 deals with the relationship between the ECS and national certificates of succession. Article. 62.2 relates not only to national certificates of succession, but also — as is clear from the guidance set out in the second sentence of recital 69 thereof — to all 'instruments available under [the] Regulation' which heirs are free to use. Therefore, Advocate General Szpunar did not consider that the determination of jurisdiction over procedures for issuing national certificates of succession solely under art. 4 of the Regulation meant that the use of the ECS was in practice mandatory.

The conclusion of Advocate General Szpunar and the decision of the CJEU that jurisdiction under art.4 on the basis of the last habitual residence also includes questions as to national certificates, is not surprising bearing in mind the purpose of the Regulation. The Polish Government and the EU Commission supported this view. It is interesting that the German, French and Portuguese Governments opposed this view and that the referral to the CJEU was necessary in the first place. Many member states are still having difficulty in coming to terms with the wide-ranging effects of the Regulation.

It is clear that no authority within member states can insist that a court document be produced instead of the ECS. However, the interaction between the use of the ECS and the collection of tax may sometimes limit their immediate practical effect.

Furthermore, thought needs to be given to the relationship between art.63.2 and the *effects* provisions of arts.69.3 and 69.4. These enable persons to rely on certificates unless they know that their contents are not accurate.

In the CJEU case of *UE and HC v Vorarlberger Landes- und Hypothekenbank AG, in the Estate of VJ,*[115] the Austrian bank refused to pay out against a Spanish ECS, on the basis that it stated that it was expressed to be unlimited in time, whilst art.70 states that certified copies are to be valid for a limited period of six months.

The court pointed out that the original ECS held by the competent authority can be unlimited in time, and that it is only the certified copies that are time limited. In this case the court held that the certified copy of the ECS was valid for a period of six months from the date of its issue,

---

[115] C-301/20

even though silent on the point.

Also it found that under art.65.1, the ECS was binding on all parties even if only requested by one of them.

The interplay between an ECS and property registers was considered in the case of *RJR v Registru Centras*[116] which is dealt with in chapter 19.

ECS are issued by the relevant authorities of participating Member States. The UK (and other third States and non-participating Member State, such as Ireland) is not able to issue an ECS. An ECS issued under the Regulation will not have any effect in the UK. However an ECS may be accepted in England and Wales (the position in Scotland or Northern Ireland may be different) by the HMCTS as evidence of foreign law for the purposes of Non Contentious Probate Rule 30 and obtaining an ECS, preferably in English, can be a cost-effective way of fulfilling the obligations under this rule.

Some practitioners question whether an ECS can or should be an authentic instrument, which might be important for a member state such as France or Italy. It is thought that this question somewhat misses the mark, since the ECS is governed by and has the effects provided in Chapter VI of the Regulation. The fact that an ECS is or is not actually an authentic instrument is therefore thought to be irrelevant.[117] However, issues relating to authentic instruments are considered in chapter 11.

---

116 C-354/21

117 See the Opinion of AG Szpunar in *Oberle* C-20/17 at para. 90.

CHAPTER THIRTEEN

MATRIMONIAL AND REGISTERED PARTNERSHIP PROPERTY REGIMES

Überschuss und Verknappung?

Feast and Famine under the Regulation

As discussed in chapter 3, the boundaries between succession law and property rights are one of the most difficult areas for the Regulation.

Since 1882, marriage in England & Wales has not affected property rights. Before, then the property of a married woman vested automatically in her husband unless it had previously been settled. Other legal systems have dealt with the property rights of married couples in very different ways. In the USA states influenced by Spanish law, the matrimonial home is very often subject to community property rights. Most civil law legal systems impose a form of community property over a wider array of property automatically on marriage unless the parties opt for a different form of matrimonial property regime. It is only the legal regimes of such places as Catalonia, Valencia, Balearic Islands and Monaco that may not do so.

In addition, the doctrine of common debts arising out of some community matrimonial property regimes, may mean that each spouse can be liable for a share of common debts. This is often the reason that spouses choose not to be subject to a community regime, for fear of liability for a share of the debts of the other spouse.

Some systems such as France permit the parties fairly free choice as to the details of the regime that they wish to choose, whilst other systems may only permit a limited number of choices. The mechanism for making a choice may also vary considerably from a formal notarial act to a "tick-the-box" exercise at the marriage ceremony.

Until it can be established what property is owned by a deceased spouse on death and their share of common debts to be deducted, it is not possible to start the succession process.

Unsurprisingly, matrimonial property regime law and succession law in a particular system, usually dovetail. The Napoleonic Code, gave succession rights to blood relatives. Spouses were therefore generally unprotected under succession law, but were protected either as independent heirs from their own family or under the legal community regime. Under the German civil code, succession rights were split between the spouse and blood relatives, so that less protection was given under the legal matrimonial regime.

However, as families and assets start to move across borders, the succession rights and the matrimonial property regimes become disconnected and produce examples of the widow's feast or famine problem. If different laws apply to the matrimonial property regime, then the surviving spouse may end up with nothing or little under both the matrimonial provision and under the succession law (famine) or alternatively too much under both (feast).

The EU Property Regime Regulations on the property effects of marriage 2016/1103,[118] and with registered partnerships, 2016/1004,[119] are beyond the scope of this book. The Property Regime Regulations deal with the usual PIL questions of jurisdiction, recognition and enforcement and applicable law. The proposals are gender neutral but the different treatment of marriage and of registered partnerships should be carefully

118 http://eur-lex.europa.eu/legal-content/EN/TXT/PDF/?uri=CELEX:32016R1103&rid=15

119 http://eur-lex.europa.eu/legal-content/EN/TXT/PDF/?uri=CELEX:32016R1104&rid=1

noted. The transitional provisions mean that the Property Regime Regulations are fully effective since 29 January 2019, but the parts relating to applicable law only apply to marriages or partnerships made after that date or to regimes amended after that date.

These two enhanced co-operation regulations are in force in 18 Member States (Austria, Belgium, Bulgaria, Croatia, Czech Republic, Cyprus, Finland, France, Germany, Greece, Italy, Luxembourg, Malta, Netherlands, Portugal, Slovenia, Spain and Sweden). Estonia may also intend to join in.

The Property Regime Regulations give one or more of the 18 states that have opted in, jurisdiction over property in that part of the EU. The interaction with the Succession Regulation is somewhat unclear particularly if a Member State is bound by the Regulation but not by 2016/1103 and 2016/1104.

Two problems on the interaction between the Regulation and the property regimes generally have become apparent, although more issues may emerge.

German Civil Code

The CJEU case of *Mahnkopf*[120] relates to Arts.1(1) and 68(1) regarding the scope of the Regulation and its boundaries with matrimonial property regimes. The issue referred being that under German law, different regimes trigger different succession law rights and thus where should the boundary between succession and matrimonial property lie.

The facts of *Mahnkopf* could not have been simpler. Lutz Mahnkopf died on 29 August 2015, 12 days after the Regulation become fully effective, leaving a widow Doris and a son Sven. Doris and Lutz were German nationals and resident there. They did not have a marriage contract and

[120] C-558/16

Lutz did not leave a Will. All of his assets were in Germany apart from a half share of a property in Sweden.

The German legal matrimonial regime (*Zugewinngemainschaft*) is one of separation of property but with equalisation of gains. On winding up the regime, the difference in value of each spouse's property at the time of winding up from that at the time of the marriage is calculated and equalised by one spouse making a transfer to ensure that each spouse has identical gains. The process can be complex and may require inventories and full disclosure.

On death, a surviving spouse is entitled to a quarter share of the estate. By Para.1371(1) of the *Bürgerliches Gesetzbuch* (German civil code, the "BGB"), the process of the equalisation of gains is simplified by merely increasing the surviving spouses share from a quarter to a half. This may have the result of giving the surviving spouse more or less than they would have been entitled to under the formal inventory route. This provision can be overridden by Will or Inheritance Contract, in which case the equalisation of gains is calculated normally and does not apply if the surviving spouse is not an heir. The question was whether the provisions of Para. 1371(1) BGB are matters of matrimonial property regimes and outside the scope of the Regulation under art.1.2(d) or matters of succession law and within the scope of the Regulation. Para.1371(1) clearly applied to all of the German assets but it was not clear that it applied to the Swedish property and therefore there was uncertainty as to what the European Certificate of Succession should state.

Notwithstanding that para.1371(1) is found within the part of the BGB dealing with matrimonial property, and in marked distinction to many academic opinions, AG Szpunar was clearly of the opinion that para.1371(1) relates to the division of the estate after death and therefore for the purposes of the Regulation, is a matter of succession, not matrimonial property law. His analysis is of interest and also discusses questions of qualification and adaptation. He also refers to the Property Regime Regulations. The CJEU agreed with AG Szpunar. All the signs are that the CJEU wants to give the Succession Regulation the widest possible scope and implement its objectives.

French Civil Code

France is unusual in permitting couples a fairly free choice as to the details of the regime that they wish to choose, usually by a formal notarial act or marriage contract.

Universal Community is defined by Article 1526 of the French Civil Code. Article 1524 sets out that the matrimonial contract may allocate the entire community to the survivor of the couple, either for the benefit of one only of the spouses, or for the benefit of whichever one survives. The spouse who thus retains the whole of the community is obliged to pay all its debts. It may also be specified that the survivor will only receive a usufruct over the share of the deceased, rather than full ownership.

Historically, these provisions have been regarded as matters of matrimonial property law in France. Whilst, art.1.2(g) also excludes property transferred by way of survivorship of joint property, there is now some uncertainty as to the boundaries of these questions. One can envisage circumstances in which all or most of the property of a marriage comes from a much older spouse and that such survivorship provisions in favour of a much younger poorer spouse may be subject to clawback, as discussed in chapter 18. If, however, the survivorship provision only applies to a very narrow range of property or there are other artificialities, particularly if the survivorship provision is for the benefit of one of the spouses only, it is conceivable that the provision might then be characterised as a matter of succession rather than matrimonial property.

For tax purposes, the transfer of property by such a survivorship is dealt with very differently under different systems. In France, such matrimonial transfers have not been subject to succession tax, whilst in Germany they have. Although tax classifications may have limited relevance, no doubt, the CJEU will have to address the whole question at some point. It is to be hoped that the CJEU finds a way to stop tax classifications unfairly affecting succession.

CHAPTER FOURTEEN

COMMORIENTES, CLASSIFICATION AND SURVIVORSHIP

Commorientes or simultaneous death is rare but still occurs particularly in disasters; tsunamis, aeroplane crashes and terrorist attacks hit the headlines, but the families directly affected then are faced with this issue.

Although, by art.1.2 (c) "questions relating to the disappearance, absence or presumed death of a natural person" are excluded from the scope of the Regulation, the CJEU decision in C-292/08 *German Graphics Graphische Maschinen GmbH v van der Schee* is authority that exclusions should be interpreted narrowly not broadly, and thus that this exclusion is a narrow one, relating solely to the question of whether a natural person is dead or alive. The connecting factors for such questions, outside the scope of the Regulation are likely to be those relating to the personal law of the natural person; either nationality for civil law states or domicile for common law ones.

By contrast *commorientes* is squarely within the scope of the Regulation.

The common law presumption is that no one of two or more people to die simultaneously or in circumstances where the order of death cannot be ascertained is deemed to have survived the other. How this presumption applies to a joint tenancy is clearly tricky.

Although survivorship provisions are excluded from the scope of the Regulation by art.1.2(g) this exclusion is somewhat circular. Since it excludes "property rights, interests and assets created or transferred otherwise than by succession, for instance by way of gifts, joint ownership with a right of survivorship, pension plans, insurance contracts and arrangements of a similar nature" and is always "without prejudice to point (i) of Article 23(2)".

Therefore, it is perfectly possible that the circumstances of the creation of a survivorship clause on the ownership of property, might be characterised as a matter of succession rather than matrimonial property under art.1.2(d) or property rights under art.1.2(g). National succession and property law, will have its impact.

Section 184 of the Law of Property Act 1925, by contrast to the common law presumption, provides that "where two or more persons have died in circumstances rendering it uncertain which of them survived the other or others, such deaths shall (subject to any order of the court), for all purposes affecting the title to property, be presumed to have occurred in order of seniority, and accordingly the younger shall be deemed to have survived the older in which the order of deaths cannot be established, then for the purposes of transfer of title, the younger shall be deemed to have survived the elder." By s.209 the Act extends to England & Wales only. The position in Northern Ireland and other jurisdictions may continue to be that no one person is deemed to have survived the other.[121]

On one view, this question is one of property law applying to all property in England & Wales, whether movable or immovable. But what does "for all purposes affecting the title to property" actually mean?

The case that is usually cited is *Re Cohn*[122] relating to the deaths of a mother and daughter in London in an air raid. The order of their deaths

---

121 See Sheila Grattan's article Options to Purchase, STEP Journal November 2017. "An old decision of Lord Thurlow to the effect that it is the 'heirs' of each of the joint tenants who take as joint tenants (not tenants in common) has influenced most academic commentary. The conventional wisdom is that the residuary legatees or the statutory next of kin of the two deceased joint tenants take as joint tenants. However, the matter is far from clear."

122 [1945] 1 Ch 5

was uncertain and could not be proved. They were, however, found to be still domiciled in Germany and the court held that the question of whether English or German presumptions should apply should be classified as a matter of succession law, rather than one of evidence in the *lex fori.* Whether the question might be one of property law and how the restriction under s.209 limited the succession law was not considered.

Article 32 of the Regulation is, it is understood, the only provision of the Regulation that affects substantive internal law rather than private international law. It states that: "Where two or more persons whose successions are governed by different laws die in circumstances in which it is uncertain in what order their deaths occurred, and where those laws provide differently for that situation or make no provision for it at all, none of the deceased persons shall have any rights to the succession of the other or others."

The article creates certainty rather than fairness. Presumably it is only if there is uncertainty as to the time of death relative to another that the presumptions in relation to such order of deaths are then to be classified as a matter for the relevant succession law. If it is known that two persons died simultaneously, then it could be argued that art.32 does not apply.

However, the problems created by the exclusions in art.1.2 of the Regulation and the limitation of the Law of Property Act and other 1925 legislation to that of England & Wales are likely to become more interesting. These limitations may well be ignored in an EU Member State if it has universal jurisdiction under arts. 4 or 10 of the Regulation.

CHAPTER FIFTEEN

WILLS, AGREEMENTS AS TO SUCCESSION AND OTHER DISPOSITIONS OF PROPERTY UPON DEATH

It is on the subject of Wills that mismatches of classification and different timings for connecting factors are perhaps most in evidence. Under the PIL of England & Wales it is often domicile at the time of an event such as the making of a Will[123] or marrying that will be the connecting factor. Under the Regulation, the connecting factor is more likely to be the law applicable to the succession as at the particular date, but sometimes on an earlier or later date. These mismatches make this chapter perhaps the most complex and difficult in this book.

Under art.3.1(d) of the Regulation, Wills, Joint Wills and Agreements as to Succession, are lumped together and defined as Dispositions of Property upon Death ("DoPuDs"), but the treatment of Wills and Joint Wills is somewhat different to that of Agreements as to Succession. The admissibility, substantive validity and binding effects of an Agreement as to Succession is governed by art.25 whilst the admissibility and substantive validity of all other DoPuDs is dealt with in art.24.

Article 3.1(b) defines an Agreement as to Succession, as "an agreement including an agreement resulting from mutual wills, which, with or without consideration, creates, modifies or terminates rights to the future

[123] For example, Rule 156 of Dicey, Morris & Collins: "A will is to be interpreted in accordance with the law intended by the testator. In the absence of indications to the contrary, this is presumed to be the law of his domicile at the time when the will is made."

estate or estates of one or more persons party to the agreement". Article 3.1(c) defines a Joint Will as "a will drawn up in one instrument by two or more persons". A mutual Will would therefore only be a Joint Will if it were created in one instrument.[124]

Therefore, whilst all wills are likely to be testamentary dispositions for the purposes of the 1961 Hague convention, HccH11, some wills are also Agreements as to Succession. A mutual will can be both a Will and an Agreement as to Succession, although the mutual agreement resulting from mutual wills may not necessarily be in writing, and the formal validity of such mutual agreement would then be outside the scope of the Regulation, whilst the formal validity of the wills themselves would be within the scope of the Regulation or HccH11.

However, the term 'Will' in the Regulation like that of 'testamentary disposition' in HccH11 is not defined. This can cause some difficulties.

Conditional gifts, survivorship rights, assurance vie, pension trusts and other will substitutes

Alternatives to wills exist in many different forms. The most common is some form of life insurance arrangement or *assurance vie*. However, many other substitutes exist, from conditional gifts, contracts with third parties, donation mortis causa, joint accounts, or accounts or property with set destinations, nominations for death lump sums, to *fideicommissum*, usufructs, trusts and foundations. Many will substitutes may be revocable, but some can be irrevocable. Some transfer property rights immediately whilst others only do so on death.

---

124 Katharina Hilbig-Lugani has written about the application of art.24 rather than art.25 to joint wills (confusingly sometimes translated from the German as "mutual wills") in The Joint Will in German-French Conflict of Laws – a stepchild of the Succession Regulation; IPRax: ISSN 0720-6585, Vol. 34, No.6,2014,pp. 480-486

There is perhaps a dichotomy between the more common law approach to will substitutes being seen as complimentary and a tool additional to wills and the more civil law approach of suspicion towards such substitutes, being seen as in some way attempting to circumvent or evade the norms of succession or tax. The distinction between testator autonomy on the one hand and protection of the family and society on the other is sharply demonstrated.

The civil lawyer may generally regard the will substitute as a nuisance, precariously built on shaky legal ground and would therefore classify them either as a will or as a gift and therefore bring them into traditional succession mechanisms.

However, this simple dichotomy between wills and gifts is not accurate. The Regulation has extended the DoPuD to include within the very broadly defined Agreement as to Succession, many will substitutes, such as mutual wills and proprietary estoppel.

The law of England & Wales is familiar with the concept of a conditional gifts by way of a *donatio mortis causa.* Other legal systems have similar conditional gifts such as the French *donation entre epoux,* but they can be made at any time and not merely when death is in sight.

However, art.1.2(g) specifically excludes from the scope of the Regulation, "property rights, interests and assets created or transferred otherwise than by succession, for instance by way of gifts, joint ownership with a right of survivorship, pension plans, insurance contracts and arrangements of a similar nature...."

Generally, the law of England & Wales would classify a French *donation entre époux* as a testamentary disposition whilst for the Regulation it and a *donatio mortis causa* would be classified as gifts and usually excluded from the scope of the Regulation. However, it is generally gifts with an immediate proprietary effect[125] that are excluded. A *donation entre époux*

125 See para.41 of the Waters Explanatory Report for HccH32

relating to the gift of a future estate may well be within the definition of an Agreement as to Succession[126]. Similar issues arise for property passing under a joint tenancy or other rights of survivorship. These would usually be excluded from the scope of the Regulation. Notwithstanding the CJEU decision in *Mahnkopf*[127], an attribution clause of the entire universal community under article 1524 of the French Civil Code will also usually be outside the scope of the Regulation.

In most states, much personal wealth is held in structures such as pension trusts, *assurance vie*, and accounts with automatic designations. These are often directed by means of letters of wishes or other will substitutes. Many such assets will also be outside the scope of the Regulation.

However, the definition in art.1.2(g) is somewhat circular, since whether or not a right is transferred by succession, is precisely the issue in question. Paragraph 46 of the Waters Explanatory Report for HccH32[128] makes it clear that all will substitutes were to be excluded from the scope of HccH32. The Regulation, however, has opened the door to will substitutes included within the definition of an Agreement as to Succession. The CJEU may in the future push at that door further.

However, it should be remembered that for the purposes of clawback under art.23.2(i) dealt with in chapter 18, the applicable succession law can include rights of beneficiaries not only against other beneficiaries but also against third parties in relation to property received both within and without the scope of the Regulation, since art.1.2(g) is expressed to be subject to such rights. Thus, although a gift itself may be outside the scope of the Regulation, the rights of beneficiaries to a clawback claim

---

https://www.hcch.net/en/publications-and-studies/details4/?pid=2959&dtid=3

126 See para.93 of the Waters Explanatory Report

127 C-558/16

128 See note 3

may still be available.

Validity

Many of the words and expressions used in the Regulation, look familiar, but *faux amis* or false cognates abound. The safest assumption is to look at each expression anew, and assess whether it has a specific definition and as to the meaning assigned to it.

In relation to wills, what is meant by validity can be confusing since it comes in many shapes and forms.

Validity of Form

Validity as to form for testamentary dispositions is generally governed by HccH11, which overrides the Regulation by virtue of art.75 (further discussed in Chapter 23). For those Member States such as Italy and Portugal that have not ratified HccH11, the question of formal validity of all written DoPuDs (because the formal validity of oral DoPuDs is outside the scope of the Regulation[129]) is governed by art.27. Article 27 also applies to all written DoPuDs that are not testamentary dispositions for the purposes of HccH11. Article 27 therefore applies to all Agreements as to Succession, other than mutual wills.

Article 27.3 also states that any provision of law which limits the permitted forms of a DoPuD by reference to the age, nationality or other personal conditions of the testator or of the persons whose succession is concerned by an Agreement as to Succession shall be deemed to pertain to matters of form.

HccH11 is specifically referred to in art.75.1. It is a convention that is in force in over 40 states, and effective in the United Kingdom by virtue of

---

[129] Art.1.2(f)

the Wills Act 1963, but it has not been ratified by all EU Member States.

Article 75.2 states that, notwithstanding that art.75.1 sets out that the Regulation shall not affect the application of international conventions, the Regulation "shall, as between Member States, take precedence over conventions concluded exclusively between two or more of them in so far as such conventions concern matters governed by this Regulation".

Since HccH11 has been ratified by numbers of states that are not EU Member States, it has not been concluded exclusively between two or more Member States and therefore it does still have precedence over the Regulation. Thus, HccH11 will still apply both inside and outside the European Union.

It should however be remembered that under art.1.2 (f), the question of formal validity of any DoPuD made orally, is outside the scope of the Regulation. Article 10 of HccH11 also permits a specific reservation on this issue and for EU Member States, that reservation applies to Belgium, Estonia, Luxembourg and France and also to the Netherlands but only in relation to citizens who are Dutch nationals only.

There are, however, other reservations and declarations in HccH11.

Article 12 of HccH11, permits contracting states to exclude any testamentary clauses which under its law do not relate to succession. Austria and Luxembourg have used this reservation. This will be the historic local definition of succession rather than the very broad one in the Regulation. Matters such as guardians for children or funeral wishes might be within this definition. The question as to guardians for children, is clearly outside the scope of the Regulation (art.1.2) but whether details of funeral arrangements may be included within the scope of the applicable law particularly in relation to the powers of heirs, executors and administrators (art.23.2.f) is not so clear.

In 1969, Poland objected to the application of HccH 11 by the West German government to West Berlin. Presumably, this objection collapsed with the Berlin Wall.

HccH11 only applies to the formal validity of testamentary dispositions (For the purposes of the Regulation, Wills and Joint Wills and not Agreements as to Succession other than mutual wills). The term is not defined in HccH11. Article 27 of the Regulation deals with the formal validity for all DoPuDs including, not only Wills, but also Agreements as to Succession; the latter other than mutual wills, being outside the scope of HccH11. The definition of a Joint Will is virtually identical under Article 4 of HccH11 as a testamentary disposition made by two or more persons in one document and art.3.1(c) of the Regulation as a Will drawn up in one instrument by two or more persons. It should also be recalled that the definition of habitual residence for the purposes of the Regulation will be a narrow EU-wide definition for the purposes of the Regulation only (and will be different from the definition used in other EU Regulations), whilst for HccH11, each contracting state may apply its own definition as to the meaning of both habitual residence and testamentary disposition.

For example, as referred to above, a French *donation entre epoux* may be classified in the United Kingdom as a testamentary disposition whilst in France it may be classified as a conditional gift, and under the Regulation as an Agreement as to Succession.

The EU member states that have not ratified HccH11 are Bulgaria, Cyprus, Czechia, Hungary, Italy, Latvia, Lithuania, Malta, Portugal, Romania and Slovakia.

Matters relating to the formal validity of all DoPuDs, for these member states will be governed by art.27 of the Regulation. Similarly, for all EU member states (other than Denmark and Ireland) matters relating to the formal validity of DoPuDs that are not testamentary dispositions will be governed by art.27 of the Regulation and not by HccH11.

Quite what a DoPuD may be, that is made in writing is not entirely clear. HccH32 refers to an Agreement as to Succession being created in writing, whilst art.1.2(f) excludes DoPuDs made orally and art.27 refers to one made in writing. Whether satisfying requirements for writing under English, Scottish or Northern Irish law, would be sufficient, is not certain. Paragraph 90 of the Waters Report set out that for HccH32, 'created in writing' should be contrasted with 'evidenced in writing'. "If an agreement had only to be proved by a writing, it could be orally created and the writing originated at some other time. All the writing would have to do is establish that an agreement was in fact entered into, and at the time alleged. To the contrary, an agreement which has to be 'created in writing' means precisely that the bringing into existence of the agreement must be by way of a document of some kind. Article 8 is not to be understood as encompassing any orally created agreement, even if proof in writing of its creation is available."

It would be hoped that the CJEU would construe the exclusion more narrowly, so that evidenced in writing might be sufficient.

Article 83.3, considered below, deals with the formal validity of a DoPuD made before 17 August 2015,

Admissibility and Substantive Validity

In the Regulation, substantive validity is a completely separate issue from that of material or essential validity. Article 24 deals with the admissibility and substantive validity of DoPuDs other than Agreements as to Succession which are dealt with under art. 25. A will which is also an Agreement as to Succession is regulated by art.25 not art.24.

Article 24.1 makes the anticipated applicable law the one to govern these questions, rather than the actual eventual applicable law. It will be the law of the habitual residence on the date of the Disposition or the national law on that day if validly chosen.

Perhaps, somewhat unnecessarily, art.24.2 enables a testator to choose a different law to govern the admissibility and substantive validity of the

DoPuD provided that it is one that could be chosen under art.22. Thus, a testator with multiple nationalities could choose one national law as the applicable succession law and a different national law to govern the admissibility of the DoPuD, or could choose a national law to govern the admissibility even though no choice was made for the applicable succession law.

Whilst admissibility is not defined, art.26 sets out (but presumably not exclusively) that matters of substantive validity for the purposes of arts.24 and 25 include such issues as

(a) the capacity of the person making the DoPuD to make such a disposition;

(b) the particular causes which bar the person making the DoPuD from disposing in favour of certain persons or which bar a person from receiving succession property from the person making the disposition;

(c) the admissibility of representation for the purposes of making a DoPuD;

(d) the interpretation of the DoPuD;

(e) fraud, duress, mistake and any other questions relating to the consent or intention of the person making the DoPuD.

Most of these are fairly clear, but are often not matters thought of by practitioners as being those of substantive validity, which is often otherwise equated to material or essential validity. This is not the case in the Regulation.

Article 26(c) is not entirely clear, but probably concerns the consent of or representation by a parent, guardian or attorney.

The provision that has caused confusion is that of art.22.3 which refers to the exercise of a *professio juris* (dealt with in chapter 21)

> and states that "The substantive validity of the act whereby the choice of law was made shall be governed by the chosen law." Recital 40 makes it clear that, "A choice of law under this Regulation should be valid even if the chosen law does not provide for a choice of law in matters of succession. It should however be for the chosen law to determine the substantive validity of the act of making the choice, that is to say, whether the person making the choice may be considered to have understood and consented to what he was doing. The same should apply to the act of modifying or revoking a choice of law."

The drafting of art.22.3 relating to the substantive validity of a *professio juris* is somewhat strange. There is no definition of substantive validity for these purposes, since art.26 only applies to arts. 24 and 25. Article 22.2 makes it clear that any such choice of law must be made in a DoPuD. One might therefore conclude that art.22.3 is somewhat superfluous. I would suggest that whilst it is unfortunate that art.26 did not expressly state that it also applies to art.22, it should be deemed to do so. The logic for the insertion of art.22.3 is that whilst under arts.24 and 25 it is possible for a different law to apply, art.22.3 makes it clear that it is always the law of the *professio juris* that will apply for the purposes of considering questions as to capacity, fraud, duress and other matters that the Regulation characterises as matters of substantive validity. This still means that a *professio juris* is still valid under the Regulation, even though such a choice is not available under the internal law of the law chosen.

Article 83.3 deals with the admissibility and substantive and formal validity of a DoPuD made before 17 August 2015 and that it will be admissible and valid both as to substance and to form, if either it meets the conditions set out in chapter III, or it is valid under the private international law rules in force at the time of the disposition in:

- the state of the habitual residence of the deceased, or

- in any of the states of the deceased's nationality, or
- in the Member State dealing with the succession

In the case of *UM,*[130] UM's father, a German national, entered into a contract on 22 July 1975 to transfer, upon his death to his son and daughter-in-law at the time equally, his ownership of a plot of land located in Austria, subject to certain conditions. When that contract, in respect of which Austrian law was designated as the applicable law, was concluded, all of the parties were habitually resident in Germany.

In this case Austrian law was chosen as the law which was to apply to the legal relationships between the parties, rather than being chosen with a view to governing the succession as a whole.

The Spanish government argued that this was a gift and therefore excluded from the scope of the Regulation and not a DoPud. The CJEU clearly found that the contract was an Agreement as to Succession but did not have to consider its validity, since it found that no valid *professio juris* had been made,

This case is considered further in relation to the *professio juris* in chapter 21.

Admissibility, ex lege revocation, loss and deemed revocation

Article 24.3 deals with the admissibility and substantive validity of the modification or revocation of DoPuDs other than Succession Agreements. If under art.24.2 a separate national law was chosen to govern admissibility, then that law governs the questions as to the substantive validity of the modification or revocation.

Under the law of England & Wales, the marriage of a person domiciled

[130] C-277/20

in England & Wales automatically revokes their Will. The position is the same in Northern Ireland, Australia and many Canadian provinces but not Scotland. In India marriage may revoke a person's Will, but not for Hindus or Muslims.

Divorce, dissolution or annulment of a marriage has an effect on wills in the United Kingdom and under many other legal systems.

In Scotland and some other jurisdictions such as Cyprus, the birth of a child has also affected a Will if it makes no provision for the child. The doctrine known as *conditio si testator sine liberis decesserit* introduced in Scotland in the 18th Century in the case of *Yule v Yule* (1758) Mor 6400 was abolished in 2016.[131] This rule also existed in England until abolished by section 19 of the Wills Act 1837.

In some jurisdictions, if a revoking will is itself revoked, then the earlier will can revive. This was the position in Scotland until amended in 2016.[132]

The connecting factor in the United Kingdom is generally that of the domicile at the time of the marriage. Revocation other than by a testamentary disposition is outside the scope of HccH11. However, for the purposes of the Regulation the admissibility and substantive validity of any revocation whether by means of a DoPuD or otherwise is governed by the deemed applicable law under art.24.3, which may be that of the habitual residence at the time of purported automatic revocation or amendment. Thus, a Will may be treated as revoked in one state but not so for the purposes of the Regulation.

For example, a testator is domiciled in England, and marries whilst habitually resident and owning a house and bank account in France. England would regard the Will as having been revoked at the time of the

[131] By s.6 of the Succession (Scotland) Act 2016

[132] By s.5 of the Succession (Scotland) Act 2016

marriage, but assuming that the Will does not create a valid *professio juris*, the French assets under the Regulation would devolve under the Will, and the applicable law would be that of the habitual residence at the time of death. However, any *renvoi* from England to France in relation to immovables would be accepted under art.34. Thus the Will would be revoked in England but not under the Regulation.

Similarly, the act of revocation of a will may be valid under the law of one state but not under the law of another, for example by destruction at the direction but not in the presence of the testator. If different laws apply to different assets, then the same issues may arise.

The California case of *Estate of McDaniels* (2008) 161 Cal.App.4th 458 underlines that the precise time when divorce may be effective for inheritance purposes may be at different times in different jurisdictions. The case of *Court, Grose, Parfitt and Gaff v Despallieres* [2009] EWHC 3340 (Ch) is an example of the cross-border difficulties relating to revocation by virtue of registration of a Civil Partnership. That case did not explore the question as to whether the will was valid in relation to New South Wales immovable property.

Under the law of England & Wales, if a will was last traced to the possession of the testator and is not forthcoming at his death, there is, prima facie, a presumption, in the absence of circumstances tending to a contrary conclusion, that the testator destroyed it with the intention to revoke it,[133] so that the relevant date will be the date of presumed destruction. The Regulation, however, is likely to classify the question as one of admissibility of the copy will rather than one of deemed revocation, so that the relevant date would be that of the original disposition. This may again result in the will being regarded as valid in one state but not another.

---

[133] Williams on Wills 10th edition para. 18.28

Material or Essential Validity

There is no reference in the Regulation to matters of material or essential validity. One reason is that other than the tie breaker rule for *commorientes* in art.32, the Regulation was prepared on the basis that it dealt with matters of private international law only, and did not affect the internal material succession law of Member States.

Whether a DoPuD is materially or essentially valid, i.e. whether its provisions respect and comply with the heirship or other family rights set out in the internal applicable succession law, will be a matter for the applicable law. Article 23.1(b) makes it clear that the applicable law governs matters of material or essential validity, although the terms are not specifically referred to.

Court Amended and Court Made Wills

Court powers to amend existing wills or to treat documents as valid that would otherwise not be formally or substantively valid or to authorise the valid execution of a will on behalf of an adult vary enormously. How a particular power is classified under the Regulation will also vary.

Rectification

The common law power in England & Wales to delete words from a will would no doubt be classified as a matter of interpretation and therefore within art. 26(d) of the Regulation. The statutory power to add words[134] has perhaps been extended in *Marley v Rawlings*[135] in a way that would be classified as relating to formal validity and within the scope of HccH11.

---

134 under s.20 Administration of Justice Act 1982

135 [2014] UKSC 2

The case of *Re Kelly*[136] looked at the question of rectification of a will made in Ireland. The court found it odd that that the classification of rectification had not already been considered. It held that the question was either one of interpretation or one of essential validity. For the purposes of the Regulation it would seem logical for it to be regarded as a matter of interpretation under art.26.1(d) and thus a matter of substantive rather than essential validity.

Other legal systems give their courts much more extensive powers in order to prove documents as wills that otherwise would not be regarded as formally valid, for example under s.58 Will, Estate and Succession Act (British Columbia), s.23 Wills Act (Manitoba) or s.37 Wills and Succession Act (Alberta) and similar legislation in Australian states and New Zealand. Many such decisions may relate both to formal validity and also to admissibility and to interpretation within the definition of substantive validity.

Statutory Wills

Whether a Statutory Will from England & Wales made under s.18 and Sch.2 of Mental Capacity Act 2005 (MCA2005) is admissible under the Regulation, is a question to be governed under art.24.1 by the deemed applicable succession law that would have applied if P had died on the day of the execution of the Will.[137] This may well be different to the current PIL restrictions in Sch.2 MCA2005,[138] and notwithstanding those provisions, a Statutory Will for a UK national for whom the law of England & Wales may be chosen, may well be effective under the Regulation to property outside the scope of the MCA2005. Practitioners

[136] [2020] EWHC 245 (Ch)

[137] And not the date of the court order authorising such execution.

[138] Para.4 limiting the effect of the Will to immovable property in England & Wales and to movable property of P if domiciled there. The Law Commission of England & Wales has considered Statutory Wills amongst other matters and is due to submit a Report and draft Bill in early 2025

will therefore need to consider carefully whether a *professio juris* in a British (or any other legal system) Statutory Will would be appropriate.

Privately Amended Wills

Deeds of Variation

In the United Kingdom Deeds of Variation are commonplace, but are of course a taxation fiction under ss.142-147 Inheritance Tax Act 1984. They are of course actually a gift from one beneficiary to another person, and would usually be classified as such. However, since they and particularly appointments out of trust under s.144 are not always well understood, they are sometimes classified under some legal systems as part of the succession process. Strictly, they should be excluded from the scope of the Regulation.

Disclaimers

Notwithstanding the application of s.144 of the 1984 Act, disclaimers by contrast, are not a gift by a beneficiary but a refusal to accept. The destination of the share of the estate disclaimed is not controlled by the beneficiary but passes in accordance with the applicable succession law, and is fully within the scope of the Regulation. Article 28 deals with the formal validity of any acceptance or disclaimer being valid, provided that it is valid in accordance with the applicable succession law or with the law of the state of the habitual residence of the relevant beneficiary. However, recital 33 makes it clear that in order to limit liability for debts any requirement to initiate proceedings under the succession law, must be complied with. This issue is considered further in chapter 17 and in relation to minor beneficiaries in chapter 20.

Disclaimers have been considered by the CJEU in three cases.

The case of *TN and NN v EG*[139] demonstrates the difficulties EU citizens have in dealing with estates cross-border and the assistance that the Regulation can give.

W.N., a Netherlands national whose last habitual residence was in Germany, died on 21 May 2018 in Bremen, Germany.

The succession was opened by EG, WG's widow in the Amtsgericht Bremen which, under intestacy, she was to inherit three quarters of the estate, and the nephews of WG, both of whom resided in the Netherlands, were each to inherit one eighth of the estate.

The nephews made a declaration of waiver in respect of the deceased's estate before the Rechtbank, The Hague, Netherlands, which was entered in that court's succession register on 30 September 2019.

By letter in Dutch, the nephews of the deceased submitted to the Amtsgericht Bremen copies of the documents drawn up by the Rechtbank. By letter of 3 January 2020, the Amtsgericht Bremen informed the nephews of the deceased that it had not been possible to take account of their letters and documents as they were not accompanied by a translation into German.

By letter in German, N.N. then informed the Amtsgericht Bremen that he and his brother had waived the succession in respect of the deceased's estate, that, in accordance with EU law, the declaration relating to that waiver had been registered by the competent judicial authorities in Dutch and that, therefore, no translation into German of the documents in question was required. In response, that court reiterated the need to translate the relevant documents in question and to comply with the time limits applicable to the waiver of succession.

The Amtsgericht Bremen (Local Court, Bremen) then ruled that the

139 C-167/20

nephews of the deceased were deemed to have accepted the succession.

The nephews contested that order but the Amtsgericht Bremen rejected the complaint and remitted the case to the referring court, the Higher Regional Court, Bremen, finding that, since the nephews of the deceased had not waived the succession in accordance with German procedural rules, they were deemed to have accepted that succession. It

Unsurprisingly, CJEU had no difficulty in finding that under arts. 13 and 28 a declaration concerning the waiver of succession made by an heir before a court of the Member State of his or her habitual residence is regarded as valid as to form in the case where the formal requirements applicable before that court have been complied with, without it being necessary, for the purposes of that validity, for that declaration to meet the formal requirements of the law applicable to the succession.

In *M. Ya M.*[140] M. Ya. M., a Bulgarian national, was the heir of his grandmother, M. T. G., a Bulgarian national who died in Greece on 29 March 2019. He applied to the referring court, the District Court, Sofia, Bulgaria, for the declaration of waiver made by the deceased's husband, a Greek national, to be entered in the register. The applicant produced a certificate of succession drawn up by the Bulgarian authorities, according to which the deceased designated as heirs her husband, her daughter and her grandson, the applicant.

The applicant submitted a written record produced by the Magistrate's Court, Athens, Greece stating that the deceased's husband appeared before that court on 28 June 2019 and declared the waiver of his inheritance. Furthermore, according to statements made in the application, the deceased's husband had stated that the deceased had last resided in Greece.

The referring court took the view that art.13 may trigger a conflict of jurisdiction since, under art.4 jurisdiction is determined by the place of

140 C-651/21

habitual residence of the deceased not the heir and that court may not be aware of the registration of declarations of waiver or of acceptance made before a court of the place of habitual residence of the heirs.

The CJEU found that art. 13 must be interpreted as not precluding a request for the registration of a waiver of the succession of a deceased person effected by an heir in the Member State in which he or she is habitually resident after another heir residing in the Member State in which the deceased was habitually resident at the time of his or her death, The CJEU also pointed out that until the habitual residence of the deceased was established it could not be known which court had jurisdiction under art.4 and therefore as to which court had standing to raise further questions with CJEU.

In *Ławida*[141] BA, a Polish national, was the heir of ZJ, who died habitually resident in Germany. BR was BA's adult representative but did not lodge a disclaimer in Poland within the time limits required under Polish law. BR applied in Poland for the time limit to be waived.

CJEU decided that the jurisdiction of the Polish court under art.13 was limited to receiving a waiver and did not have jurisdiction to agree changes to time limits. The German court would have universal jurisdiction under the applicable law.

Agreements as to Succession

Generally, the internal laws of countries that have some derivation from the German civil code permit inheritance contracts, whilst most other jurisdictions do not. Relatives who would normally have succession rights on death can, whilst the testator is still alive, enter into a contract, which must usually be before a notary and in the presence of the testator, agree some different form of division. A combined matrimonial property

---

[141] C-57/24

regime and inheritance contract made before marriage is not uncommon.

In France, a form of inheritance contract has been available from 2007 and in Italy an inheritance contract limited to business assets was introduced in 2006.

It was perhaps not helpful that the same German word, *Erbvertrag,* is used in both the German civil code and in the German version of the Regulation. This has caused confusion, since many German lawyers have assumed that the concepts are identical. For the purposes of the Regulation, however, an Agreement as to Succession has a much wider definition than that of a German inheritance contract.[142]

The classic English view of inheritance is that it can only relate to assets at death and that therefore proprietary estoppel (and constructive trust) claims must be determined first before the question of succession is considered. However, it is clear that the Regulation is much broader than this. The definition of an Agreement as to Succession in art.3.1(b), "an agreement …which, with or without consideration, creates, modifies or terminates rights to the future estate or estates of one or more persons party to the agreement" will clearly encompass proprietary estoppel claims. Although art.1.2(f) excludes the formal validity of DoPuDs made orally, other matters in relation to oral Agreements as to Succession, such as questions of the applicable law and their admissibility and substantive validity are still within the scope of the Regulation.

The Hon Mr J Henry Carr in the case of *Winkler v Shamoon* [2016] EWHC 217 Ch considered whether the court had jurisdiction under the old Brussels I Regulation 44/2001 or whether the matter was one of "Wills and Succession" excluded under Art.1.2(a) of 44/2001.

At paras 60 – 72 the court considered the Regulation, notwithstanding that the UK is not bound by it, as an aid to interpreting the Wills and

142 Case C-277/20 will clarify whether a particular German conditional gift in relation to Austrian immovable property is an agreement as to succession.

Succession exclusion in Brussels I and concluded that the proprietary estoppel claims took the issues out of the scope of Brussels I by virtue of the exclusion for Wills and Succession.

Paragraph 93 of the Waters Report indicates that the French *donation entre époux* would be included within the HccH32 definition of an Agreement as to Succession so far as it relates to a gift of a future estate, whereas a *donation-partage* as a gift of existing property would not be within the definition. These paragraphs of the Waters Report are helpful both in understanding the agreements that are likely to be included in the definition and also the common law perspective in which such agreements have historically not been included.

The CJEU case of *UM143* referred to above indicates that the court is likely to take a broad view.

Admissibility, Substantive Validity and Binding Effects

As set out above, substantive validity is a completely separate issue from that of material or essential validity. Article 25 covers the admissibility, substantive validity and binding effects of Agreements as to Succession, including agreements resulting from mutual wills, and in the same way as art.24 refers these questions (also including conditions for its termination) to the deemed applicable succession law if the party to the agreement had died on the day that it had been made. Article 25.2 deals agreements covering the succession of more than one person.

Article 26 sets out that matters of substantive validity for the purposes of art.25 is the same as for art.24 referred to above.

However, art.25 also refers to the binding effects of an Agreement as to Succession and clearly deal with the contractual and non-contractual rights and obligations between the various parties to the Agreement. Recital 50, however makes it clear that any succession rights under the

143 C-277/20

final applicable succession law take preference over a valid DoPuD including an Agreement as to Succession. However, a valid *professio juris* (see chapter 21) made in an Agreement as to Succession can continue to be effective under art.22.

Registration

The establishment of national systems for Will registration and communication of information was encouraged by the Council of Europe under the Basel Convention no.77 of 16th May 1972 on the Establishment of a Scheme of Registration of Wills. Convention 77 is in force in Belgium, Cyprus, Estonia, France, Italy, Lithuania, Luxemburg, Netherlands, Portugal, Spain, Turkey and the Ukraine.

The Convention although signed and effected by sections 23-25 Administration of Justice Act 1982, has never been brought into force in the United Kingdom. Germany and Denmark have also signed, but not yet ratified.

The *Association du Réseau Européen des Registres Testamentaires* (ARERT) [the European Network of the Registers of Wills (ENRWA)] has been building gradually and now provides links to the registers in Austria, Belgium, Bulgaria, Estonia, France, Germany, Greece, Hungary, Latvia, Luxembourg, Netherlands, Poland, Romania and Slovakia. Croatia, Estonia, Italy, Portugal and Slovenia, Spain and Switzerland are also members of ARERT. The links vary from full connectivity to electronic request. Czechia, Denmark, Lithuania, Sweden, Finland, and Ireland are not currently involved. http://www.arert.eu/Information-sheets.html gives useful details of registration and searching Will registers throughout the European Union.

Belgium, France, Luxembourg and the Netherlands also include European Certificates of Succession (see chapter 12) on their registers.

Pressure for an EU wide system of registration and search for wills continues to grow. It is very likely that some recognition of the existing

ARERT and ARERT LITE models will become the norm. The registers will become the place where other facts relevant to succession can also be registered; not only ECS, but matrimonial property regime contracts, conditional gifts and agreements as to succession.

CHAPTER SIXTEEN

ADMINISTRATION, ADMINISTRATORS AND EXECUTORS

From a common law perspective, the Regulation is somewhat quiet on the subject of administration. Article 23.1(f) includes "the powers of the heirs, the executors of the wills and other administrators of the estate in particular as regards the sale of property and the payment of creditors, without prejudice to the powers [dealt with below] referred to in Article 29.2 and 29.3".

In the UK, administration is a matter of procedural law separate from the material applicable inheritance law and administration is therefore governed by the *lex fori,* and not by the connecting factors for inheritance. In most systems in the EU, administration is not regarded as a separate legal category from inheritance but part of the overall classification of succession. The knowledge that any reference in the Regulation to 'succession' also includes administration, helps an overall understanding.

It is axiomatic that an English (or Scots or Northern Ireland) Grant is required to administer all assets situated in England & Wales, other than the statutory exception for life insurance policies. Separate grants are of course required in each UK jurisdiction if the deceased died domiciled outside the UK. *Haji-Ioannou (Deceased) and others v Frangos*[144] is an interesting judgment setting out the distinctions in the private international law of England & Wales between inheritance and administration for the purposes of the registration of a judgment under Brussels I, Regulation 44/2001, and supporting the contention that

[144] *[2009] EWHC 2310 (QB)*

whilst UK PIL may apply *renvoi* to inheritance it does not do so to administration.

Generally, all regimes that treat movable and immovable property identically ('unitarian') may require all assets sited in their own jurisdiction, to be administered in their own jurisdiction, whilst regimes that differentiate between movable and immovable property ('schismatic') may regard movables which are subject to the succession law of the deceased's patrimony as also being subject to administration by that patrimony. Lawyers in those jurisdictions can become angered and perplexed by the separation of the forum from the estate – the classification of administration as being separate from succession.

Other unitarian and schismatic jurisdictions will regard matters of administration differently. Generally, the concept of Executors or Administrators, if it exists at all, is very different. In many civil law jurisdictions title passes direct to the heirs (under the doctrine of *seisin*) who can either renounce or accept their inheritance. Acceptance and renunciation and liability for debts is considered in the next chapter.

In Denmark, Finland and Sweden (as in the United Kingdom and Ireland) estates are administered by the personal representatives who take possession of assets, settle liabilities and then remit the residuary estate to the beneficiaries. In Austria, Italy and Spain, heirs must accept the estate, in order to obtain it and in Austria they have must also obtain a court probate. In Belgium, France, Luxemburg, the Netherlands, Germany and Greece, heirs take automatically under the doctrine of *seisin* which gives them the automatic right to take possession of the estate and the authority to exercise the rights of the deceased. In some states such as Spain and Germany, administrators may be appointed but their powers may be limited.

Different legal systems, have differing ways of establishing status as a personal representative:

- In the United Kingdom and Ireland and other common law jurisdictions a grant of representation relating to the powers of the administrator or executor of the will is issued by the court.

- In Denmark, administration is mainly carried out by the court. Nevertheless, if beneficiaries agree to accept liability for debts, they may themselves administer the estate and must in this case draw up an inventory submitted for the approval of the court.

- In Sweden, successors evidence their rights by means of an inventory drawn up in the presence of two persons of good faith. The inventory is obligatory. It validates the contracts signed between one of the persons shown there with the status of heir or legatee and third parties.

- In Finland, an inventory is drawn up, which provides a list of the heirs and legatees and may be certified by the office responsible for maintaining the register. Third parties of good faith who sign contracts with the persons mentioned in the inventory are protected.

Prior to the Regulation, different Member States used different connecting factors for administration. In Austria administration was regarded as being subject to Austrian law if administration took place in Austria, in the Netherlands to Dutch law if the deceased had his habitual residence in that country, and in Portugal to the personal national law of the deceased. All of these rules have been overtaken by the Regulation to the extent that a matter is within its scope.

A personal representative under the law of England & Wales must administer assets according to that law, whether the administration is principal or ancillary, and is entitled to hold the assets against a personal representative in another jurisdiction, even if the assets are received from that state.

A personal representative in another jurisdiction must administer assets according to the administration prescribed by that state, and is entitled to hold the assets against a personal representative under a grant from England & Wales.

Even if there are no other personal representatives, the England & Wales personal representative is, generally, under no duty to collect non-UK assets, whether movable or immovable, but is, however entitled to try to collect assets sited in another state and is accountable for all such assets actually collected.

If the deceased died domiciled in England & Wales, the England & Wales personal representative may be under a duty to seek such assets, if there are insufficient assets in the UK to pay the debts of the deceased. If there are sufficient assets to meet the debts, the England & Wales personal representative is not under any such duty. In such case, personal representatives, may if they wish leave the matter of foreign assets to the others, so that they would have to be responsible for any foreign tax and collection costs. If the personal representative does collect foreign assets, any expenses, whether foreign tax, transport costs or insurance must fall on a specific legatee and not on residue.

These aspects of the law of England & Wales do not sit well with the Regulation.

The case of *Haji-Ioannou (Deceased) and others v Frangos*[145] illustrates the fundamental differences between UK PIL and the way that the Regulation is to work.

> "I do not accept the further argument advanced by Mr Layton that the moveable asset was the right to have the judgment registered in England and that this is located in England. As Mr Millett points out in his skeleton, it would mean that anyone who died with the benefit of an unsatisfied Community judgment had property in

[145] *[2009] EWHC 2310 (QB) paras.72 and 73*

> every EU jurisdiction. In accordance with English law, it is only property situated in England which automatically vests in the personal representative. Movables out of the jurisdiction only vest in the representative if they are brought into England: "any moveables of the deceased which after his death are brought into England before any person has, in a foreign country in which they are situate, obtained a good title thereto under the law of such foreign country (*lex situs*) and (*semble*) reduced them into possession." (*Dicey* (2006) Rule 132 (2) 26R-021).

Moveable property of the deceased located abroad will not vest in an English administrator or personal representative and in any event will not do so if a person has already obtained good title to it.

However, these are the separate PIL rules that the UK applies to administration. Within the SR Zone, the Regulation is now applied. Whether or not the PIL rules of the UK are accepted under the Regulation depends upon the interpretation of art.34 as set out below.

Article 29 and Special Rules for Administrators

As in Ireland and the UK, the appointment of administrators is compulsory in Cyprus. In Sweden and Finland an administrator must be appointed if a beneficiary requests it. Under other systems, the courts may require the appointment of an administrator.

Article 29 deals with the position if a Member State such as Cyprus has jurisdiction, but the appliable succession law is that of another state, which does not appoint administrators or whose administrators have lesser powers. The article as explained in recital 44 requires the courts of the state with jurisdiction to respect the applicable succession law, but permits the appointment of an administrator where necessary and permits additional powers to be granted by way of exception.

The article was drafted very much with the possibility in mind that Ireland or the UK might decide to opt in to the Regulation in the future. The commentary on the original draft regulation stated: "The aim of this Article is to take into account the specific features of common law legal systems, such as the English legal system, where the heirs do not directly acquire the rights of the deceased upon the latter's death but where the succession is managed by an administrator appointed and supervised by the judge."

Renvoi

It well understood that the Administration of Estates Act 1925 (and other aspects of administration under the law of England & Wales) is limited in scope to England & Wales. This has sometimes been interpreted as meaning the details of administration of an estate outside the United Kingdom under the law of England & Wales, should not include the 1925 Act. However, it is clear that s.58 limiting the extent of the Act to England & Wales only, is intended not to step on the toes of other parts of the United Kingdom. The Act does not apply to the administration of estate assets in Scotland. The Act follows the general PIL rules for administration within the UK and many common law systems and applies the law of *situs* to administration.

As described in chapter 22, art.34 makes it clear that under the Regulation *renvoi* can be accepted. If the applicable succession law is that of a third State, the private international law rules of that third State are included, in so far as they make a *renvoi* to the law of a Member State or to the law of another third State which would apply its own law. However, under art.34 no *renvoi* is to apply to various matters including those under an art.22 *professio juris*.

Therefore, if there is no *professio juris,* then administration of assets within the SR Zone are to be administered under the local law, if such is the PIL of the state of habitual residence. A person dying habitually resident in the UK with assets outside the UK whether movable or immovable is to have such assets administered under the local law, even though movable assets may be subject to the inheritance law of the place of habitual residence.

However, if there is a valid *professio juris,* it is to bring with it the whole of that law and *renvoi* is not to apply. As set out in recital 42, "The law determined as the law applicable to the succession should govern the succession from the opening of the succession to the transfer of ownership of the assets forming part of the estate to the beneficiaries as determined by that law. It should include questions relating to the administration of the estate and to liability for the debts under the succession. The payment of the debts under the succession may, depending, in particular, on the law applicable to the succession, include the taking into account of a specific ranking of the creditors."

Article 29 is silent in relation to the powers of administrators in a Member State where such powers do not usually exist. Recital 44 however makes it clear that "The powers exercised by the administrators appointed in the Member State of the court seised should be the powers of administration which they may exercise under the law applicable to the succession. Thus, if, for instance, the heir is appointed as administrator he should have the powers to administer the estate which an heir would have under that law."

It seems extremely doubtful that the CJEU would not find that if the law of England & Wales is chosen under a valid *professio juris,* the administration of the entire estate would be governed by the administration law that would apply to assets within England & Wales; i.e. that s.58 AEA1925 would be classified as a matter of PIL and therefore *renvoi* and disapplied by art.34.

However, it is difficult to see how the Regulation can impose any obligation on England & Wales personal representatives to administer assets outside the UK. If there is a valid *professio juris,* so that England & Wales administration law will apply in the SR Zone and the UK personal representatives choose not to administer assets in the SR Zone, then ancillary administrators who are so willing would need to be appointed, in the Member State with jurisdiction. Clearly there will be practical difficulties in doing so and in many cases adaptation in one form or another as described in chapter 19 will be required.

CHAPTER SEVENTEEN

DEBTS, THIRD PARTIES, DISCLAIMERS AND LIMITATIONS

Under art.23(g) of the Regulation, the applicable succession law governs the liability for the debts of the estate (although estate is not defined). The French version refers to the *des dettes de la succession* (succession is defined) and the German to *die Nachlassverbindlichkeiten* (Estate liabilities, which are not defined).

Article 23(f) also makes the applicable succession law govern the powers of the heirs, executors and administrators as regards the payment of creditors but without prejudice to the special powers for administrators given by art.29 for states such as Cyprus, referred to in the previous chapter.

Different succession laws treat the obligations to pay creditors very differently. Whilst in the UK the obligation to settle the debts of the deceased is a personal obligation of the personal representatives but is limited to the assets of the estate, under other laws, the obligation will usually vest in the heirs who may be liable for the debts of the deceased without limit, unless they take particular steps to limit their liability. Historically, people in some civil law jurisdictions could therefore become bankrupt by being the heir of a bankrupt deceased.

In addition, the doctrine of common debts arising out of some community matrimonial property regimes, if the deceased died subject to such a matrimonial property regime, may mean that a spouse is liable for some of the deceased's debts or the deceased for some of the spouse's debts. This should have been clarified in the prior winding up of the deceased's property regime.

The applicable succession law will therefore govern questions as to the time limits for creditors making claims, whether personal representatives or heirs are jointly and severally liable or only jointly liable and the rights between personal representatives or heirs to reimbursement between them.

Assets in the hands of the England & Wales personal representative are available to pay all debts of the deceased, whether in the UK or elsewhere. The personal representative must follow the order of priority of debts as prescribed by the law of England & Wales.

If non-UK creditors have already been paid, the personal representative should adjust payment, so that creditors in England & Wales receive an equivalent proportionate amount, before foreign creditors receive further payments.

There is no duty on an England & Wales ancillary personal representative to advertise for foreign claims, but there may be such a duty on a personal representative of a deceased dying domiciled in England & Wales. S.27 Trustee Act 1925 gives protection to personal representatives, who distribute after advertising "in the Gazette, and in a newspaper circulating in the district in which the land is situated and such other like notices, including notices elsewhere than in England and Wales, as would, in any special case, have been directed by a court of competent jurisdiction in an action for administration."

Advertising outside the UK ought perhaps now to be more common.

Acceptance and Limitation of Liability

Article 28 deals with the formal validity of an "acceptance or waiver of the succession, of a legacy or of a reserved share, or a declaration designed to limit the liability of the person making the declaration". Such a declaration is formally valid if valid under either the applicable succession law or under the law of the State in which such a person has their habitual residence. It should be noted that this is not limited to a Member State.

Accordingly, for individuals habitually resident in, for example, England & Wales, a form of disclaimer of either executorship or a legacy or of residue in England & Wales law form is formally valid.

However, recital 33 purports to limit the formal validity declarations made under the law of the habitual residence of the relevant beneficiary or personal representative and makes it clear that if the applicable succession law requires court or inventory proceedings in order to limit liability, then a mere declaration under the law of the habitual residence will not be regarded as formally valid. It is questionable as to whether a mere recital really does limit the effect of art.28, but clearly it would be prudent to comply with the wording of recital 33 where feasible so that, if the applicable succession law would make beneficiaries liable to the debts of the deceased without limit, it is prudent to take steps under that law to limit that liability.

Local advice is required, but acceptance by an heir with the benefit of an inventory is the usual mechanism for limiting such liability. There are however often strict time limits which must be complied with and ensuring that the inventory is comprehensive can be difficult. The inventory is sometimes certified by bailiffs who are not used to including assets or debts outside the jurisdiction. Careful but prompt thought as to the full effects of universal jurisdiction is necessary.

Jurisdiction

As discussed in chapter 9, universal jurisdiction under the Regulation is given under art. 4 to the Member State of the deceased's last habitual residence with subsidiary jurisdiction under art.10 based on nationality or habitual residence in the previous 5 years. Jurisdiction based on the situs of assets is limited to those assets.

No jurisdiction exists solely on the basis of the place of a creditor.

If an estate is solvent, the position of creditors under the Regulation will therefore very much depend upon whether any Member State does or does not have universal jurisdiction under arts. 4 and 10. If no such universal jurisdiction exists, creditors must continue to take their chances under the various PIL rules of the third States involved.

However, personal representatives in the United Kingdom, will always be well advised to ensure that they either have the protection of s.27 of the Trustee Act or a suitable court order in relation to distribution notwithstanding an awareness of a potential claim. Beneficiaries will of course still be subject to potential tracing claims.

Insolvent Estates

Insolvent estates are always difficult and in England & Wales can be administered either under bankruptcy or under the Administration of Insolvent Estates of Deceased Persons Order 1986 No. 1999.

Article 76 of the Regulation makes it clear that the EU Insolvency Regulation[146] can still apply even if the debtor has died. Different member states have differing rules, and the Insolvency Regulation takes precedence in relation to matters of jurisdiction and applicable law ahead of the Regulation. Jurisdiction is given to the centre of the debtor's main interests, which may be different to that of the last habitual residence, and generally, the law of the forum is applied.

146 For matters post 2017, (EU) 2015/848 of 20 May 2015 on insolvency proceedings

CHAPTER EIGHTEEN

OBLIGATIONS TO RESTORE, CLAWBACK, COLLATION AND REDUCTION

I am very grateful to Jayne Holliday for her 2020 book Clawback Law in the Context of Succession,[147] which has brought much information on this subject together for the first time.

Like the term "Forced Heirship", "clawback" carries the hint of a common law sneer; the sort of nonsense that civil law systems would get up to, wouldn't they.

Generally, under systems with stronger and more far reaching inheritance rights, the requirements for the formal validity of wills may be lower and *vice versa*. England & Wales with supposedly lower rights for family members has a higher hurdle for internal formal validity of dispositions. By contrast, unwitnessed holographic wills are a usual feature of many civil law systems. Similarly, under systems with stronger and more far reaching inheritance rights, the anti-avoidance provisions preventing steps to get around obligations to restore are also more far reaching. Clawback brings back into the estate lifetime gifts in order to calculate the size of the share of the estate to which beneficiaries are entitled and obliges donees to return assets or contribute money in order for succession rights to be met.

The issue of clawback is not a unique problem for common law systems such as England & Wales. Clawback in one form or another already exists under UK insolvency legislation and also, although not often invoked, under the 1975 Act and the 1979 N.I. Order with six year time limits.

[147] Hart ISBN 978-1-50993-232-0

The Divorce courts however have no difficulty in using and enforcing clawback against parties attempting to shield assets from their powers.

In practice, this issue affects most EU Member States, many of which have very different rules for life-time gifts to heirs and to non-heirs. In the Netherlands, clawback is limited for gifts to non-heirs made within the 5 years before death and is a monetary claim rather than a claim to the asset itself. In France, there are no time limits and the value of the asset is that as at the date of death. In Italy the claim is to the asset itself with no time limits.

Many Member States, such as Czechia, Denmark, Estonia, Finland, Hungary, Lithuania, Malta, Slovakia and Sweden give family members full succession rights but do not consider life-time gifts to be part of the estate and under their own law do not operate clawback from third parties.

As suggested by Holliday, the distinction between obligations to restore from life-time gifts to heirs, which she names Collation, and to non-heirs, that she names Clawback, needs to be made explicit. French law distinguishes between *Rapport* or Reversion and *Reduction* or Set-Off. Generally, Reversion binds heirs, whilst Set-Off can bind both heirs and non-heirs.

The obligation for heirs to bring back into account gifts that they have already received or separate gifts under the DoPuD under collation are not problematic. English doctrines of advancement and hotchpot are not controversial. HccH32[148] made it clear that it included collation rules, but not clawback.

There is however an inherent tension within the Succession Regulation. Article.1.2(g) excludes "property rights, interests and assets created or transferred otherwise than by succession, for instance by way of gifts, joint ownership with a right of survivorship, pension plans, insurance

148 Article 7.2 (c) and para.78 Waters Report

contracts and arrangements of a similar nature, without prejudice to point (i) of Article 23(2)" from the overall scope.

Article 23.2(i) on the scope of the applicable succession law includes "any obligation to restore or account for gifts, advancements or legacies when determining the shares of the different beneficiaries".

It can be argued that art.23(i) only includes the obligation to restore within the scope of the applicable law for the purposes "when determining the shares of the different beneficiaries" and not including any obligation on third parties to restore. However, the list of matters within art.23 is not exhaustive, so that obligations on third parties to restore could be within the scope of the applicable law. The key question is whether such an obligation could be within the overall scope of the Regulation. One would hope that CJEU would agree that such property law matters are outside the scope of the Regulation.

If the Regulation did extend its scope and the scope of the applicable succession law to include all forms of clawback, this could be extremely problematic. Life time gifts to third parties could in the future become subject to different clawback rules by virtue of a change of habitual residence of the donor prior to death.

The original draft of the Regulation stated that "the exclusion of rights and properties created or transferred other than by means of succession to the estates of deceased persons covers not only the forms of joint property [joint tenancy] known under *common law*, but also all forms of gifts under civil law."

The distinctions between succession law, property law, and maintenance law, are here very blurred. Under English law the case of *Gorjat v Gorjat*[149] is of interest in considering the gift of movable property outside

[149] [2010] EWHC 1537 (Ch)

the UK and whether the Rome I regulation might apply to enforceable gifts.

Holliday outlines the detailed negotiations on the issue of Clawback that took place prior to the finalisation of the Regulation. Compromises were proposed and negotiated, but eventually without any agreement. At one point the Presidency responded to a proposal that claims against third parties who had acquired property from the original done were outside the scope of the Regulation. The Commission also accepted that clawback from third parties who have acquired the property from the original donee was on the border between succession and property law and if anything lay more towards substantive property law".[150]

Even if such arguments were accepted by CJEU this would still leave original donees at risk to claims of which they might have had no knowledge at the time of the gift. A person in Estonia might have no idea that if the donor moved to Italy, that a claim to a right in rem might continue to exist whenever the donor died.

Such a position is unsatisfactory. It may be that CJEU will limit the scope of the applicable law under art.23.2(i). Certainly, from a common law perspective, the exclusion in art.1.2(g) would give CJEU the ability to draw a clear line between property rights of third parties and the succession rights of beneficiaries.

Attempting to protect donees is not straightforward. The primary protection is to ensure that the place of the gift and the relevant assets is in a jurisdiction that will not enforce any clawback. All potential beneficiaries can be asked to waive their rights using an inheritance contract if available or any other suitable form of agreement as to succession, in order to provide some form of estoppel in writing. Additionally, donors could be asked in suitable circumstances to contract into a choice of their national law under art.22 and bind themselves not

150 Holliday p.104

to change it. Nothing is currently fool-proof, but any protection may be better than nothing.

This subject will not go away.

CHAPTER NINETEEN

PROPERTY LAW AND ADAPTATION

Paragraph 4.1 of the Explanatory Memorandum states that 'The publication of property rights, in particular the functioning of the land register and the effects of an entry or failure to make an entry in this register, is also excluded' which is effected by art.1.2(k) and (l) which distinguishes between the exclusion of the nature of rights *in rem* on the one hand and the recording in a register of such rights (of both movable and immovable property) and the effects of such recording.

The number and length of the relevant recitals, 15 -19, indicates the political difficulties that shaped the negotiation of these provisions.

The nature of Rights in *Rem*

Recital 15 makes it clear that although the "Regulation should allow for the creation or the transfer by succession of a right in immovable or movable property as provided for in the law applicable to the succession" it "should, however, not affect the limited number ('*numerus clausus*') of rights *in rem* known in the national law of some Member States. A Member State should not be required to recognise a right *in rem* relating to property located in that Member State if the right *in rem* in question is not known in its law."

As described in chapter 3, in many legal systems, the recording of rights is definitive. All owners must be registered and if not registered, they have no rights. The nature of those rights is tightly defined and the types of rights limited to a specific number of types of right. It was intended that the Regulation should not trespass onto the individual property law systems of Member States. However, as ever, clear boundaries between succession rights and property rights are not always easy to find or maintain across different systems.

Some writers distinguish between the acquisition of the right *in rem* which are generally governed by the Regulation and the content and effects of the right *in rem* which are not.

The CJEU decided the matter of *Fundación Gala-Salvador Dalí*[151] before the Regulation came into effect, and in that case that Directive 2001/84/EC on resale rights did not preclude national law reserving the benefit of the resale right to the artist's heirs at law alone, to the exclusion of testamentary legatees. The CJEU accordingly sent the matter back to the French court to take due account of all the relevant rules for the resolution of conflicts of laws relating to the transfer on succession of the resale right.

Subject to the application of the art.30 exception set out in chapter 7, it would now be clear under the Regulation that the applicable succession law would govern the acquisition of such resale rights rather than the artist's heirs at law inheriting under the specific rules of the French civil code.[152]

Adaptation

Although art.1.2(k) is not expressed to be without prejudice to art.31 and adaptation of rights *in* rem, Recital 16 goes on to make it clear that notwithstanding recital 15, "in order to allow the beneficiaries to enjoy in another Member State the rights which have been created or transferred to them by succession, this Regulation should provide for the adaptation of an unknown right *in rem* to the closest equivalent right *in rem* under the law of that other Member State. In the context of such an

[151] C-518/08

[152] Article L. 122-7 of the Intellectual Property Code

adaptation, account should be taken of the aims and the interests pursued by the specific right *in rem* and the effects attached to it. For the purposes of determining the closest equivalent national right *in rem*, the authorities or competent persons of the State whose law applied to the succession may be contacted for further information on the nature and the effects of the right. To that end, the existing networks in the area of judicial cooperation in civil and commercial matters could be used, as well as any other available means facilitating the understanding of foreign law."

Article 31 requires a Member State to apply adaptation under the Regulation and in addition recital 17 makes it clear that "adaptation of unknown rights *in rem* as explicitly provided for by this Regulation should not preclude other forms of adaptation in the context of the application of this Regulation." However, art.31 cannot take effect in relation to matters that are outside the scope of the Regulation and the precise boundary between matters relating to the "nature of rights *in rem*" and adaptation of such a right other than in relation to its nature, is a grey area. Member States may be reluctant to extend adaptation under art.31 in some circumstances. Whether the CJEU will or will not force them to do so, may well depend upon the individual facts and in practice a measure of leeway may be available to Member States.

Adaptation is a widely used doctrine. As has been described in chapter 15 conditional gifts in common law systems are often limited to the narrow concept of *donatio mortis causa.* In other systems they can be extensive but in common law systems may be regarded as a form of testament.

A civil law usufruct may be adapted by employing a common law life interest trust in its place, if the usufruct cannot be employed. Similarly, a life interest trust whether under intestacy or under a DoPuD may be adapted to a usufruct in a civil law system. Scotland has a usufruct in its legal system, the proper liferent[153] but it is rarely used and accepts the concept of a trust. Quebec also has a usufruct in its legal system, but trusts

153 Referred to in s.43(4) of the Inheritance Tax Act 1984

are now often used in their place. The tax effects of adaptation are outside the scope of the Regulation and of this book, but can be considerable.

The Roman law concept of the *fidei commissum* or *Vorerb* and *Nacherb* under German and Dutch systems is again adapted to a form of trust under common law systems. It may not have a direct effect on rights *in rem* under other civil law systems since the owner's powers may not be restricted save on death.

The CJEU case of *Kubicka*[154] directly concerned the question of adaptation under the Regulation, arising out of a Polish Will affecting German immovables. Under the Polish civil code a specific legacy can either vest directly in the legatee under the doctrine of vindication or via residue so that it is becomes an obligation of the heirs under the doctrine of damnation.

Germany and the Netherlands do not recognise the doctrine of vindication and have always applied the doctrine of damnation instead.

As a result of the Succession Regulation the Netherlands has changed its law so that if a foreign law is chosen that does have the doctrine of vindication then it will be accepted. Germany by contrast changed its law to state that vindication would still not be accepted.

Mrs Kubicka, a Polish national, was still alive and wanted to ensure that the German house in which she and her German spouse lived and which they jointly owned passed to him on her death. She made a Polish will leaving her share of the house to him by way of vindication and the residue between her spouse and children.

The Polish Notary, Marcin Margonski, knowing of the German limitation refused to register the Will and Mrs Kubicka appealed.

154 C-218/16

The CJEU agreed with AG Bot that German law is incorrect and that the Polish law doctrine is a succession law matter relating to the transfer of rights *in rem* and not to the nature of the rights *in rem* themselves or to registration, and therefore within the scope of the Regulation and effective over German immovables as a result of the valid *professio juris* of Polish law.

The recording in a Register of Rights in Immovable and Movable Property

Recital 18 elaborates on the issue of recording in a register at some considerable length. 'The requirements for the recording in a register of a right in immovable or movable property should be excluded for the scope of this Regulation. It should therefore be the law of the Member State in which the register is kept (for immovable property, the *lex rei sitae*) which determines under what legal conditions and how the recording must be carried out and which authorities, such as land registers or notaries, are in charge of checking that all requirements are met and that the documentation presented or established is sufficient or contains the necessary information. In particular, the authorities may check that the right of the deceased to the succession property mentioned in the document presented for registration is a right which is recorded as such in the register or which is otherwise demonstrated in accordance with the law of the Member State in which the register is kept. In order to avoid duplication of documents, the registration authorities should accept such documents drawn up in another Member State by the competent authorities whose circulation is provided for by this Regulation, in particular, the European Certificate of Succession issued under this regulation should constitute a valid document for the recording of succession property in a register of a Member State. This should not preclude the authorities involved in the registration from asking the person applying for registration to provide such additional information, or to present such additional documents as are required under the law of the Member State in which the register is kept, for instance information or documents relating to the payment of revenue.

The competent authority may indicate to the person applying for registration how the missing information or documents can be provided.'

The decision of CJEU in *RJR v Registrų centras VĮ*[155] somewhat limits the scope of this recital. In that case the deceased died habitually resident in Germany. RJR was the sole heir and obtained an ECS that confirmed this. The Lithuanian Land Registry refused to register RJR as the new owner of immovable property there, since the ECS did not identify any property. CJEU confirmed that the Regulation did not preclude legislation in a Member State rejecting an ECS which did not identify the relevant immovable property.

Revenue matters are of course outside the scope of the Regulation by virtue of art.1.1.

Recital 19 deals with the exclusion of the effects of the recording of a right in a register. 'It should therefore be the law of the Member State in which the register is kept which determines whether the recording is, for instance, declaratory or constitutive in effect. Thus, where, for example, the acquisition of a right in immovable property requires a recording in a register under the law of the Member State in which the register is kept in order to ensure the *erga omnes* effect of registers or to protect legal transactions, the moment of such acquisition should be governed by the law of that Member State.'

The local requirements for dealing with national registers, whether of land or of other assets, will usually take precedence. However, the ECS and its effects are governed by the Regulation and as in the CJEU case of *Oberle*[156] considered in chapter 12, requirements for a national certificate of inheritance may be overridden.

155 C-354/21

156 C-20/17

European Judicial Network in civil and commercial matters (EJN)

The **EJN** has published some information sheets[157] on national law which explain:

- the rights *in rem* that could arise from a succession
- whether such rights are recorded in a register of rights in immovable or movable property
- the effects arising from their registration
- specific rules and procedures for adapting a right *in rem*.

[157] https://beta.e-justice.europa.eu/486/EN/adapting_rights_in_rem

CHAPTER TWENTY

CHILDREN AS BENEFICIARIES

It is in relation to minor children that the differences between common and civil law systems are most stark. In many states assets can be owned by minors and inherited assets must pass directly to them if they are heirs, even though they are under age.

As detailed in chapter 18, generally the types of rights *in rem* in lcgal systems are limited and in civil law systems, registration is usually paramount. The registered proprietors are the owners for all purposes. In civil law systems, property is usually held by minor children directly. Under common law systems, by contrast, property for minor children is usually held by others for their benefit, The registered proprietors may not be the owners for all purposes.

Similarly, as detailed in chapter 16, whilst in most common law systems, the debts of a deceased are limited to the assets of the estate, in some civil law systems, heirs can inherit the burden of debts in their entirety over and beyond the value of the assets of the estate.

A child in the United Kingdom whose parents own a property in France can be affected by the succession provisions under French law giving the child an automatic right to receive a certain proportion of the French property (which vests directly in the child) even since the Regulation became fully effective on 17 August 2015, and despite the child being a UK citizen and habitually resident in England and Wales. In contrast, in England and Wales, the estate of a deceased person will pass to a personal representative to hold the property for the child until it reaches 18.

Conversely, consideration may have to be given to renouncing an inheritance where, as in many civil law jurisdictions, as a result of the local law, a child as an heir would become responsible for all of the debts of the deceased, if the child does not renounce.

There are many issues which need to be considered, whether dealing with the acceptance or renunciation of an inheritance or the sale of a property. The issues obviously differ, depending on the jurisdiction involved, but some are considered below.

As detailed in chapter 3, the laws of another jurisdiction may still be relevant, for example, when English PIL creates a *renvoi* back to French law in relation to immovable property in France or if a UK resident minor inherits assets from someone habitually resident in an EU Member State.

Jurisdiction

Under the EU Brussels II *ter* Regulation,[158] fully effective since 1 August 2022, Article 7.1 gives the courts of a Member State jurisdiction in relation to matters of parental responsibility over a child who is habitually resident in that Member State at the time the court is seised. For third States, Article 5.1 of HccH 34, referred to below, gives the courts of the Contracting State of the habitual residence of the child jurisdiction to take measures directed to the protection of the child's person or property.

Brussels II *ter*, only deals with matters of jurisdiction and not questions of the law that will be applicable.

[158] Council Regulation (EU) 2019/1111 of 25 June 2019 on jurisdiction, the recognition and enforcement of decisions in matrimonial matters and the matters of parental responsibility, and on international child abduction .

Applicable Law

Less straightforward is the question of which law the court seised must apply. One might conclude the law of the country of the court with jurisdiction.

One criticism of many regimes for adults with incapacity is that they can be inappropriately treated as children. For children, the criticism can be that they are all treated the same, whether they are aged 7 or 17. The UK Supreme Court in *In the matter of LC (Children)*[159] refers to both Brussels II *bis* and HccH 34[160] on Jurisdiction, Applicable Law, Recognition, Enforcement and Co-operation in respect of Parental responsibility and Measures for the Protection of Children of 19 October 1996. HccH has published a very useful practical handbook on HccH 34.[161]

HccH 34 has been ratified by all EU Member States. Article 3(g) provides that the administration, conservation or disposal of the child's property is within the scope of such protective measures, while Article 15(1) states that in exercising their jurisdiction under the provisions of Chapter II, the authorities of the Contracting States shall apply their own law.

The difficulty with such an analysis in the present context is that Article 1(3)(f) of Brussels II *bis* and Article 4(f) of HccH 34 exclude trusts and successions from their scope. Matters are further complicated by the fact that different elements of a country's law come into play, for example in relation to rights and procedural issues.

It might be assumed that matters of capacity (i.e. the right to inherit or the procedural ability to inherit) in relation to succession would be governed by the Regulation.

---

159 [2014] UKSC 1

160 https://www.hcch.net/en/instruments/conventions/full-text/?cid=70

161 available at http://www.hcch.net/index_en.php?act=publications.details&pid=6096&dtid=3

However, legal capacity concerning the right to inherit is construed very narrowly. Thus, conditions on the *right* to inherit, or conditions on the capacity required in order to *exercise* succession rights, are matters for the applicable succession law. For example, if the relevant succession law requires authorization by a minor's legal representative, or judicial approval, it will be governed by the Regulation.

However, ascertaining the identity of the legal representative (e.g. the person authorised to sign documents on the child's behalf) does not relate solely to succession law. This is a *general* question of capacity (i.e. a legal procedural ability to complete the necessary legal steps to achieve something), regulated not by the Regulation, but by Brussels II *bis* and the HccH34 (since it falls outside the scope of trusts and succession for the purpose of these instruments).

For example, it would follow that the powers of a parent or guardian to accept or renounce succession or deal with that child's property are therefore a matter for the courts of the state in which the child is habitually resident, under Brussels II *bis* and HccH34.

European Case Law

These issues were considered in the case of *Matoušková* (C-404/14) and the conclusion was reached that the approval of the division of an estate was a matter of parental responsibility, falling within the scope of Article 1(1)(b) of Brussels II *bis*, and not a measure relating to succession excluded under Article 1(3)(f).

Whilst each case will turn on its facts, and a different application might cause the Court to reach a different conclusion, it is worth noting the comments of the Court that where two issues are so closely related (as is often the case with distinct elements of this type of application), it "*would not be appropriate to apply different jurisdictional rules*". As such, the sale of a foreign property might be seen as the key element of a Court application, while the acceptance of succession is incidental to that sale.

The judgment of the CJEU of 6 October 2015 in *Matoušková* C-404/14 decided that the approval of an agreement for the sharing-out of an estate concluded by a guardian *ad litem* on behalf of minor children constituted a measure relating to the exercise of parental responsibility within the Brussels II *bis* Regulation No. 2201/2003 and not a measure relating to succession. It perhaps showed some of the limits to the Regulation.

Families experience real life problems as a result. The estate of a deceased may be in, say, the Czech Republic, but if the minor beneficiary is habitually resident in England & Wales, the courts with jurisdiction in parental responsibility matters will be the English courts, and under HccH 34 must generally apply the law of England & Wales. The need to obtain approval from the court dealing with guardianship matters is a direct consequence of the status and capacity of the minor children and constitutes a protective measure for the child relating to the administration, conservation or disposal of the child's property in the exercise of parental responsibility within the meaning of Articles 1(1)(b) and 2(e) of Brussels II *bis*.

However, the decision in *Matoušková* was given at a time when the Regulation had only recently become fully effective and the jurisprudence has since developed. The whole issue was revisited by the CJEU in its decision in *Saponaro* C-565/16 made on 19 April 2018. The facts underline the problems involved and again show why action on behalf of a minor beneficiary is often required in a European cross-border succession.

Mr Sapanaro and Ms Xylina, acting on behalf of their minor child, made an application to the Small Claims Court, Leros, Greece for authorisation to renounce the inheritance from Ms Xylina's late father, the maternal grandfather of that child. The deceased died intestate on 10 May 2015. At the date of his death, he was living in Greece. His estate comprised movables located in Greece worth EUR 900 in total. However, the deceased had been convicted of attempted fraud and his heirs were liable to be the subject of a civil action for damages brought by the victim. The deceased's wife and daughters, the grandmother, mother and aunt of the minor child, had already renounced their inheritance, since otherwise, they could be personally liable to the victim of the deceased. The father and mother of the minor child applied, on behalf of the latter to whom the inheritance fell, for authorisation to renounce it.

Mr Sapanaro and Ms Xylina and their minor child were habitually resident in Rome, Italy and therefore the Italian courts would normally be thought to have the relevant jurisdiction for the minor child. However, prorogation or transfer of jurisdiction may be possible under Article 12(3) of Brussels II *bis* in relation to parental responsibility "where the child has a substantial connection with that Member State and the jurisdiction of the courts has been accepted expressly or otherwise in an unequivocal manner by all the parties to the proceedings at the time the court is seised and is in the best interests of the child.

The CJEU decided that the joint lodging of proceedings by the parents of the child before the courts of their choice was an unequivocal acceptance by them of the jurisdiction of that court; that the prosecutor who, according to the national law, was a party to the proceedings and silence as to the prorogation might be regarded as implicit consent; and the fact that the residence of the deceased at the time of his death, his assets and liabilities were all situated in the Member State of the chosen courts meant that prorogation of jurisdiction was in the best interests of the child.

The judgment leads to some interesting conclusions and questions. The implied acceptance by the parents does not seem to be controversial. Again, the notion of a tacit consent by failing to object, would not seem to be overtly controversial. It is clear however, that the victim of the deceased, was not a party to these proceedings, may also reinforce the view that creditors are not "parties concerned" for the purposes of a choice of court agreement under art.5.

The 2025 CJEU case of *Anikovi*[162] is also very helpful in analysing the issues involved, under Brussels II *ter*. In this case, M. I. A., the mother of two minors, E. M. A and E. M. A, requested authorisation from the Bulgarian court to sell, the shares they owned in three immovable properties in Bulgaria. All three parties were Russian nationals habitually resident in Germany.

The CJEU confirmed that the request to sell the shares owned by that minor in immovable property situated in another Member State came within the scope of parental responsibility, within the meaning of Article 1(1)(b) of Brussels II *ter*, in that the authorisation concerned protection measures, as referred to in Article 1(2)(e), with the result that, pursuant to Article 7(1), it is the courts of a Member State in which the minor is habitually resident at the time the court is seised which, in principle, have jurisdiction to grant that authorisation.

CJEU noted that Article 10(1) of Brussels II *ter*, headed 'Choice of court', provides that the courts of a different Member State shall have jurisdiction in matters of parental responsibility where:

(a) the child has a substantial connection with that Member State,

(b) the parties, as well as any other holder of parental responsibility have and accepted the jurisdiction of the court; and

(c) the exercise of jurisdiction is in the best interests of the child.

The referring Bulgarian court could therefore assume jurisdiction under the Brussels II *ter* provided that it ensured (i) that, in the context of the proceedings brought before it, there was a concrete and significant connection between Bulgaria and the personal interests of the child concerned, as could be the case bearing in mind that that child owned a share of immovable property situated in that Member State, (ii) that, given that in non-contentious proceedings, there is no defendant party,

162 C-395/23

the mother of the minor, as the sole holder of parental responsibility, expressly accepts the jurisdiction of that court in the course of the proceedings after having been informed of her right not to accept it, and (iii) that the exercise of that jurisdiction is in the best interests of the child.

Law of England & Wales

The law of England & Wales in relation to the powers and duties of parents and guardians for minor children is set out in the Children Act 1989.[163] Section 3(3) of that Act states that Parental Rights "include, in particular, the right of the guardian to receive or recover in his own name, for the benefit of the child, property of whatever description and wherever situated which the child is entitled to receive or recover." Under English law, therefore, there is a parental right to accept assets, but no explicit right to accept liabilities on behalf of the child nor any explicit right to dispose of the child's assets.

The effect of this is that (under the law of England & Wales that a court in England & Wales would apply under Brussels II *ter* and HccH 34) a minor child habitually resident in England & Wales, cannot itself accept or renounce a foreign succession. Taking, again, the example of France, a child cannot accept or renounce a share in a French estate, nor partition or sell French property. Similarly, although a parent has the right to accept the inheritance, they are at risk in relation to any liabilities or if they attempt to authorise any partition or sale. A court order would be necessary at the very least in order to protect the parent.

---

163 Available at http://www.legislation.gov.uk/ukpga/1989/41/contents

Application

Historically, under the civil law PIL of most EU member states, capacity has been a question governed by the child's personal law being the law of the state of the child's nationality, whereas for common law states the personal law of a child is usually that of the law of the state of the child's domicile (as defined under the relevant common law rules).

This meant that a child with UK citizenship, most closely connected to England & Wales, was regarded by civil law states as being subject to English law on capacity, whereas common law states would look to the law of the child's domicile (which may not necessarily coincide).

Now, however, for those states subject to Brussels II *ter* and HccH 34, a child is subject to the jurisdiction of the courts in the state in which he is habitually resident and those courts will apply their own law, save in relation to matters that are particularly specific to the succession insofar as they come within Article 1(1)(b) of Brussels II *ter*, as matters of parental responsibility.

Despite the fact that a minor cannot own or deal with property, the English High Court has jurisdiction to make an Order permitting the sale of the asset, in order to hold the sale proceeds for the benefit of the child. In order to obtain the necessary Order, an application must be made to the High Court - usually the Chancery Division.[164]

Assuming the Order is granted, the person authorised to accept or disclaim the inheritance or to sell the property can do so or if authorised, sign a form of power of attorney to enable the acceptance, disclaimer or sale to be effected. Occasionally, if circumstances change or matters have not been fully considered at the time of the original hearing, the matter will have to return to Court. For example, if assets belong to the minor, the child will ordinarily have the right to call for assets to be transferred to him when he reaches 18. However, the child may reach the age of 17

164 Under Parts 8 and 64 of the Civil Procedure Rules

and it may be thought inappropriate to transfer the assets at 18 owing to the minor's lack of maturity and the value of the assets, in which case, the trustee may wish to return to Court for further directions.

It may assist in certain circumstances to remind the Court of the alternative bases on which to found jurisdiction under Brussels II *ter* or HccH 34, for example, the nationality of a child, or the jurisdiction of habitual residence of one of their parents. This may point to an alternative or more appropriate venue.

Conclusion

In order to avoid the problems which arise in these circumstances, individuals who are considering making a gift to a minor may wish to structure it in a way which will not give rise to complications on sale, or it may be decided that property should be retained until a child reaches majority, in order to avoid the need for such an application.

For EU Member States, Brussels II *bis* Regulation was of course superseded by the Brussels II *ter* Regulation,[165] that entered into force on 22 July 2019, and which became fully on 1 August 2022. The new Article 16 (and Recitals 32 and 33) gives effective jurisdiction to other relevant courts on incidental questions. Thus, one may consider that these difficult incidental questions are now a thing of the past. However, it has been argued that (notwithstanding the new Recital 33 of Brussels II *ter*) the questions in *Matoušková* and *Saponaro,* were not incidental ones. CJEU will still have further questions to consider.

---

165 (EU) 2019/1111, of 25 June 2019.

CHAPTER TWENTY-ONE

PROFESSIO JURIS AND CHOICES OF LAW

The broad effect of the Regulation is to provide that, a person's estate both movable and immovable is universally to be subject to one law being that of the last habitual residence. However, by exercising a *professio juris*, the law of nationality may instead be chosen by a testator as the law to govern the succession as a whole.

Many existing Wills may already include a valid implied choice or be deemed to include one. In practice there are six different such choices, with possibly different effects.

Explicit (Post and Pre 17 August 2015)

Article 22 sets out that the choice of the law of nationality is valid if the deceased had that nationality either at the time of choice or at the time of death.

The effect of the words "may choose as the law to govern his succession as a whole" is not entirely clear. The safest course, may be to assume that to be effective, the choice should affect all of the assets within the succession, and that therefore one universal Will dealing with all worldwide assets containing such a choice is preferable. It could be argued that separate choices relating to separate parts of the succession by way of separate Wills dealing with assets in different jurisdictions, might not be effective. This would be a question for the courts with jurisdiction to decide and is best avoided where possible.

As discussed in chapter 15, to be sure of substantive validity, under art.22.3, it is therefore perhaps safest for such a *professio juris* to be made in a Disposition of Property upon Death (DoPuD) which is substantively valid (for the purposes of art.26) in accordance with the internal law of the State chosen and for that DoPuD to have worldwide effect.

It is clear from Recital 40, however, that there is no requirement for the chosen applicable law itself to provide for a *professio juris* in succession matters. Thus, although the substantive validity of the act is to be governed by the chosen law, the material validity of the choice is governed by the EU SR.

Although the Regulation only governs the successions of persons dying on or after 17 August 2015, the transitional provisions in art.83 give effect to choices of law and DoPuDs made before the Regulation was fully effective. Article 83.2 makes it clear that such a choice is also valid even if made before the Regulation came fully into effect on 17 August 2015.

Implicit (Post and Pre 17 August 2015)

Recital 39 sets out that a choice of law "could be demonstrated by a [DoPuD]where for instance, the deceased had referred in his disposition to specific provisions of the law of the State of his nationality or where he had otherwise mentioned that law."

Thus, a Will made using law terms from the law of England & Wales, may be an implicit choice of that law and again art.83.2 makes it clear that such an implicit choice is also valid even if made before the Regulation came fully into effect on 17 August 2015.

However, whilst an explicit choice indicates that the testator and any advisor will have considered the effects of such a choice of law and of the Regulation generally, it is highly unlikely that this would be the case under an implicit choice.

Does this therefore indicate that specific consideration by the testator of the possibility and effects of a *professio juris* is not a requirement for the choice to be valid and effective? It might be that the CJEU, may in the future hold that if it is clear that no such consideration by the testator was given, then no valid choice can have been made. In his opinion to the Court of March 26, 2020, Advocate General Manuel Campos Sánchez-Bordona stated that the implied *professio juris* resulting from a demonstration of the terms of a disposition of property upon death referred to in art. 22.2 must result exclusively from the terms of such provision and not from the general circumstances of the deceased's life.[166]

This argument may also be supported by the specific creation of Historic Deemed choices under art.83.4 referred to below.

Historic PIL

Article 83.2, does not only validate a *professio juris* under art.22 that became valid from 17 August 2015.

In addition, a *professio juris* that was valid under the private international law of either the law of the testator's nationality or habitual residence at the time of the choice, before 17 August 2015 remains valid from 17 August 2015.

Thus, previously existing choices of law available under, for example, Czech, Italian, Finnish, Dutch, German or Polish private international law or continuing ones such as under Swiss private international law, validly made before 17 August 2015 continue to be effective even though they may now no longer be available. Considering and advising on such choices of law, is therefore essential. It may no longer be possible to make such an historic choice of law, and therefore the accidental revocation of such a choice, could have unpleasant consequences for negligent advisers.

---

166 *E.E.* C-80/19 at para. 104

It should be noted that the historic choice of law in the Netherlands arose from its ratification of HccH 32 that applied solely to inheritance law issues (as defined in article 7 of HccH 32), and not administration or other matters that are within the scope of the Regulation. Therefore, an effective continuing historic choice of law under the historic PIL of the Netherlands only affects the applicable inheritance law (as defined in article 7 of HccH 32) and not other issues within the scope of the Regulation such as administration, that will be governed by the applicable law under the Regulation. This mirrors the effects of *renvoi* from many common law systems that differentiates between inheritance law and administration law as referred to in chapter 22.

As referred to in chapter 15, in the case of *UM,*[167] UM's father entered into a contract on 22 July 1975 to transfer, upon his death to his son and daughter-in-law at the time equally, his ownership of a plot of land located in Austria, subject to certain conditions. When that contract, in respect of which Austrian law was designated as the applicable law, was concluded, all of the parties were habitually resident in Germany.

The conditions set out in that contract included inter alia the obligation for UM's father to erect a house, for UM and his wife to remain married and for the latter to still be alive. The contract provided that if these conditions were not met, UM would be the sole beneficiary. UM's father also authorised the transfer of ownership to be recorded in the Austrian Land Register upon production of an official death certificate and proof that the conditions required to effect the transfer were met. Prior to the death of UM's father in Cologne, Germany on 13 May 2018, UM and his wife had divorced and she had subsequently died.

Succession proceedings were brought before the Amtsgericht, Cologne, Germany, the last place of residence of UM's father.

---

[167] C-277/20

The case of E.E.[168] made it clear that a person may choose a law 'to govern his succession as a whole' under art.22 of the regulation, and that art. 83.2 relates to cases where, prior to 17 August 2015, the deceased had chosen the law 'applicable to his succession'.

In this case Austrian law was chosen as the law which was to apply to the legal relationships between the parties, rather than being chosen with a view to governing the succession as a whole.

A disposition upon death made before 17 August 2015 by a donor who died after that date will be valid, pursuant to art.83.3, if the conditions laid down by the law designated by the provisions of Chapter III – and more specifically art.25, which applies to agreements as to succession – are satisfied, or, failing that, if it is valid under the conflict of law rules applicable prior to the entry into force of that regulation.

Article 83.2 was inapplicable, no choice having been made as to the law which was to govern the succession as a whole and art.83.4 inapplicable since the deceased would not have been able to choose Austrian law, not being an Austrian citizen.

Thus whilst the contract was a valid agreement as to succession the choice of law related only to the agreement itself and there had been no valid *professio juris* in relation to the succession as a whole.

Historic Deemed

The deeming provisions of art.83.4 are, perhaps, the most problematic. It is understood that art.83.4 was inserted in the EU Parliament late in the legislative process and therefore does not sit comfortably in the overall regulation.

[168] C-80/19

A DoPuD made before 17 August 2015 under the law of the nationality is deemed to exercise a choice of law. There are likely to be many such historic deemed choices of law that have already been made.

There is clearly no requirement that the DoPuD made under national law for the purposes of art.83.4 must relate to the whole of the succession.

However, if a testator has multiple nationalities and multiple Wills, there is no tie-breaker clause in art.83.4 and therefore no means of determining which *professio juris* takes precedence.

It is not clear if a specific choice is made under art.83.2 and also a separate deemed choice is made under art.83.4 as to which takes preference. An example, of this, might be an Italian making an Italian Will, and specifically choosing the law of his habitual residence being another state. It is presumed that a specific *professio juris* will override any deemed choice and take precedence.

In his opinion to the Court of March 26, 2020, Advocate General Manuel Campos Sánchez-Bordona made the point that if the deeming provisions of art.83.4 apply, then it is not then necessary to research into whether an actual or deemed *professio juris* under art.22 or art.83.2 have actually been made. The CJEU in its decision of 16 July 2020 found[169] that by virtue of both arts. 83.2 and 83.4 a valid *professio juris* had been made and did not specify one above the other.

On a separate point, it has also been argued by some that a Will made before the Regulation came into force on 17 August 2012 cannot be regarded as having created a deemed choice under art.83.4. However, there is no requirement in art.83.4 that such a Will must have been made after 16 August 2012, merely that it must have been made before 17 August 2015.This argument therefore appears fallacious.

---

[169] *E.E.* C-80/19 at 5)

Territorial Systems

Multi-territorial legal systems

States such as the United Kingdom, Canada, Australia and the United States of America comprise several territorial units (a law district) each of which has its own different succession laws. Under Article 36, it is to be the private international law rules of such a state that shall determine the relevant law district whose laws shall apply, but in the absence of such rules Article 36 sets out the factors in order to decide the applicable law.

For a state such as Australia with federal PIL rules these federal rules will apply under art.36.1.

However, for states such as the UK, Canada or USA where the state itself does not have such federal PIL, but relies on the PIL of each individual law district, then art.36.2 a) applies the law of the law district in which the deceased was habitually resident in relation to art.21 but art.36.2 b) applies the law of the law district with which the deceased was most closely connected to any choice under arts 22, 24 or 25. These may, of course, not be the same as the law district in which the deceased died domiciled under the local law.

Under art.36.2(b) a US citizen making a *professio juris* of US law (whether explicitly or otherwise), for the purposes of assets in the EU is under the Regulation choosing the inheritance and administration law of the US state with which they are most closely connected. Advisors, will also need to understand the concept of habitual residence under the Regulation in order to ascertain which system of law applies under art.36.2(a) if no election is made.

United Kingdom

The United Kingdom is much misunderstood, even by its citizens. For practitioners outside the United Kingdom, confusion abounds. The precise meanings of England, England & Wales, Britain, Great Britain, the United Kingdom are rarely considered when drafting. The different definitions of UK nationals are not necessarily well known, but include British Citizens, British Overseas Territories Citizens, British Overseas Citizens, British Nationals (Overseas), British Subjects and British Protected Persons.

For most EU purposes, reference to a UK national meant a British Citizen, but since the Regulation is of universal application, all categories of UK nationality are thought to be included.

Although the PIL rules of each of the UK law districts is virtually identical, it is not a national UK rule. The rule is a matter for each law district. Scotland, for example, changed some of its PIL in the Family Law (Scotland) Act 2006. Thus, the UK is in the same position as the USA. Choice of the law of nationality by a UK citizen, will not necessarily refer to the law of domicile. I may be domiciled in England & Wales, but habitually resident in or most closely connected to Scotland or vice versa. There are, no doubt, many Scots domiciled individuals, habitually resident in England. If the Regulation is in play, it may not be a question of the domicile but of the habitual residence or closest connection that decides as to the law of which part of the UK applies.

A *professio juris* may provide some surprises. For example, a Jersey or Isle of Man citizen, if most closely connected to another part of the United Kingdom including all territories under the suzerainty of the Crown, and if making a valid *professio juris* of national law, may find that they have chosen a succession law different to that intended.

The specific wording of a *professio juris* has not yet been considered by CJEU. Caution is therefore needed. Specific thought and advice will be needed on each occasion but in order to cover off all bases, wording to be considered for England and Wales might be:

> "I am a citizen of the United Kingdom, domiciled, habitually resident in and most closely connected with England & Wales. Under Article 22 of Regulation (EU) No. 650/2012, I choose the

> law of my nationality to govern my succession as a whole [and also under Article 24, this disposition] and believe that this choice is to be construed as being that of the law of England & Wales."

Inter-personal legal systems

Some states such as India, Pakistan, the Lebanon and Morocco have different systems of applicable succession law for different categories of persons, depending on their religion.

Under art.37, it is to be the rules of that state that determine which is the applicable law by virtue of a reference to the law of that State. Many such states do have clear rules. The law in India and Pakistan is set out in the Indian Succession Act 1925[170] (called the Succession Act 1925 in Pakistan). In the absence of such rules, the system of law with which the deceased had the closest connection are to apply.

It should always be remembered that a *professio juris,* whether explicit, implied or deemed, under the Regulation, brings with it the whole of that law, administration as well as inheritance.

Provided that all of that law is wanted then making an explicit *professio juris* perhaps in a combined inheritance and matrimonial contract, is always logical. Addressing the choices available under the Property Regulations in addition to that available under the Regulation would also be wise.

If however a *professio juris* is not wanted, then again, it is wise specifically to state in a valid DoPuD that no such choice is being made. Specific thought and advice will be needed on each occasion but wording to be considered and adapted might be:

---

170 http://www.districtcourtsnamchi.nic.in/laws/indian_succession_act_1925.pdf

> "I am a citizen of the United Kingdom, domiciled, habitually resident in and most closely connected with England & Wales. I do not wish to choose, under Article 22 of Regulation (EU) No. 650/2012, the law of my nationality to govern my succession as a whole [nor under Article 24, this disposition] and wish the law of the state of my habitual residence to apply including its private international law rules."

CHAPTER TWENTY-TWO

RENVOI, NO RENVOI AND LIMITATIONS OF SCOPE

Renvoi

Renvoi in general is considered in chapter 2, including the concepts of remission and transmission, but is always a difficult concept. Broadly, if the relevant connecting factor, whether habitual residence or nationality establishes that a foreign substantive law is to be applied, the question that has to be decided is whether or not the reference to the foreign law includes a reference to all of the PIL rules of that law or merely the internal foreign law with no reference to PIL.

The difficulties of *renvoi* are often conceptual. For a practitioner in a third State, it is important to work out the relevant jurisdiction in the EU under the Regulation, and consider the question of *renvoi* from the perspective of the courts of that member state. Perspectives from the courts of the third state will generally be irrelevant and may confuse.

No Renvoi and Jurisdiction

Article 34 by implication abolishes *renvoi* between member states (whether or not there is a *professio juris*) but as set out in recital 57, if the applicable law is that of a third State, the private international law rules of that third State are included, in so far as they make a *renvoi* to the law of a Member State or to the law of another third State which would apply its own law. However, under art.34 no *renvoi* is to apply to various matters including those under an art.22 *professio juris*.

Thus, the explicit choice of national law now by, for example, an Australian citizen living in Spain would be of the relevant internal state law of part of Australia and would not include its private international law rules relating to movables and immovables. Australian PIL would then be irrelevant.

Whilst for a Spanish national living in New South Wales, Australian PIL would be relevant, unless the Spaniard had made a valid *professio juris* and thus *renvoi* was excluded under art.34.

Renvoi, No Renvoi, and Article 83

However, there is no reference in art.34 to the exclusion of *renvoi* in relation to choices made under the transitional provisions of art.83.

It can probably be safely assumed that pre 17 August 2015 explicit and implicit choices will exclude *renvoi* since they are in effect made under art.22.

Historic PIL choices made under art.83.2 will carry with them their own historic *renvoi* rules. Generally, such historic PIL choices themselves excluded *renvoi* under the relevant Italian, Swiss or other PIL.

It is the deemed choices under art.83.4 that seem to be the most problematic. Article 83.4 itself does not refer to art.22. It is not clear as to whether an art.83.4 deemed choice is also to be deemed to be under art.22 for the purposes of art.34 and *renvoi*. If *renvoi* is to be excluded, it could be argued that art.34 should have been amended so as specifically to include a choice under art.83.4.

Since art.83.4 was not drafted by the EU Commission there is no evidence as to the intention of the legislature.

Similarly, it is only a valid art.22 *professio juris* in favour of a participating Member State that after death will enable the "parties concerned" to choose that State for the purposes of jurisdiction under art.5. It was uncertain as to whether this choice of jurisdiction is also available under a Historic Deemed *professio juris* under art.83.4.

As referred to in chapter 21 in the CJEU case of *E.E.*[171] Advocate General Manuel Campos Sánchez-Bordona made the point that if the deeming provisions of art.83.4 apply, then it is not then necessary to research into whether an actual or deemed *professio juris* under art.22 or art.83.2 have actually been made. The CJEU in its decision of 16 July 2020 found[172] that by virtue of both arts. 83.2 and 83.4 a valid *professio juris* had been made and did not specify one above the other. It did however, specifically confirm that the choice of jurisdiction by the parties concerned under art. 5 was effective as a result of both arts.83.2 and 83.4. This does therefore also imply that the CJEU might well view a deemed choice under art.83.4 as being also a valid choice under art.22 for the purposes of *renvoi* and art.34, so that *renvoi* would not then be accepted.

If this were not the case, then it might well be that immovable property in, for example, France would remain subject to French succession law for persons habitually resident in third States with private international law rules that direct that the law of the *situs* applies to immovables, unless such a person makes a valid explicit or implicit *professio juris* of their national law under art.22. To avoid this uncertainty, it would be wise to ensure that there is always an explicit *professio juris* rather than to rely on art.83.4

Renvoi, Scope and Limitation of Scope

There are two particular areas of complication in relation to *renvoi.*

It should be remembered that different aspects of "succession" such as inheritance or administration may have different connecting factors. Under the PIL of the UK jurisdictions, inheritance for movables will

---

171 C-80/19

172 *E.E.* C-80/19 at 5)

follow domicile but for immovables *situs*. Administration by contrast may simply follow *situs*.

Thus, the movable property in France of a person dying habitually resident in England & Wales, but domiciled in Jersey, without a valid *professio* juris, will be subject to the inheritance law of Jersey but the administration law of France. Prior to the Regulation, France might not have accepted that renvoi, but under art.34 must now do so.

The other question is whether or not a particular reference to another law, is to be classified as a matter of *renvoi* under the Regulation.

The obvious example is that of s.1(1) Inheritance (Provision for Family and Dependants) Act 1975 under which the rights to make a claim only apply to the estates of persons dying domiciled in England & Wales, so that the immovable property in England & Wales of a person dying domiciled elsewhere has been unassailable.

If the law of England & Wales applies to an estate by virtue of art.21, then *renvoi* will be accepted, so that the application of another succession law to property both inside and outside England & Wales can be accepted under art.34. However, if the law of England & Wales is applicable by virtue of a valid *professio juris* under art.22, then *renvoi* is not accepted. Is the limitation within s.1(1) a matter of *renvoi* or an entry condition? Does a valid choice of the succession law of England & Wales then apply the provisions of the 1975 Act to all assets, even though such provision may not be accepted within the United Kingdom?

Whilst many practitioners are sceptical, it should be borne in mind that the relevant court considering the question is likely to be that of the deceased's last habitual residence. It is likely that the testator chose the law of England & Wales, since the law of the habitual residence gave succession rights that the testator did not wish their estate to be subject to. It is then likely that the court would be looking closely at the question of the validity of the *professio juris,* and if satisfied that the choice was valid, then wishing to apply the whole of the succession law of England

& Wales including if claimed by the beneficiaries, the powers under the 1975 Act. This would seem to be the intention behind the Regulation; that a valid choice of law should bring with it, the whole of that law.

It has been argued that the Administration of Estates Act 1925 is limited in scope to England & Wales, so that the details of administration of an estate outside the United Kingdom under the law of England & Wales, should not include the 1925 Act. However, it is clear that s.58 limiting the extent of the Act to England & Wales only, is intended not to step on the toes of other parts of the United Kingdom. It does not apply to the administration of estate assets in Scotland. It follows the general PIL for administration within the UK and many common law systems and applies the law of situs to administration. However, for the purposes of the Regulation, a valid *professio juris* is to bring with it the whole of that law, and it is very doubtful that the CJEU would not find that in such circumstances, the 1925 Act is to apply to assets outside England & Wales; i.e. that s.58 would be classified as a matter of PIL and therefore *renvoi* and disapplied by art.34.

Similarly, the Succession (Scotland) Act 1964 removed the right of a surviving spouse to a usufruct (the widow's *terce* or the widower's *courtesy*) in one third of heritable (immovable) property on the death of a spouse. Since 1964 Scottish succession legal (as opposed to prior) rights apply only to the movable property of Scottish domiciled persons. Changes to this division have often been suggested but not yet implemented. A valid *professio juris* of Scottish law, is likely to bring with it the obligations of legal rights in relation to worldwide movables even though the deceased may not have died domiciled in Scotland.

The New South Wales (NSW) case of *Taylor v Farrugia*[173] is an interesting insight into how NSW deals with these issues. NSW retains jurisdiction for NSW immovables under the Succession Act 2006

[173] [2009] NSWSC 801 http://www.austlii.edu.au/cgi-bin/sinodisp/au/cases/nsw/NSWSC/2009/801.html

(formerly the Family Provision Act 1982) even when the deceased died domiciled outside NSW (in this case in Malta an EU member state). Brereton J, used the fact that the defendant son John Farrugia lived in Malta, whilst the plaintiffs lived in NSW, to partition the Maltese assets to John as the Maltese resident defendant, by obtaining undertakings from the plaintiffs that they would disclaim their inheritance rights under Maltese law. NSW law does not however deal with the problem of movables subject to a choice of NSW succession law.

A valid *professio juris* is likely to bring with it the whole of the chosen law, including many aspects considered by the PIL of the chosen law to be limited. Many testators particularly with a deemed *professio juris* from a will made before 17 August 2015, might be surprised that they had made such a deemed choice and the effects of such a deemed choice.

CHAPTER TWENTY-THREE

TREATIES WITH THIRD STATES

One of the issues that has only now reached the CJUE[174] is that of International Succession Treaties.

Article 75 of the Regulation contains rules that clarify the relationship between the Regulation and pre-existing conventions and treaties. Broadly, such treaties override the effects of the Regulation in various ways, whether changing the usual rules on jurisdiction or on applicable law.

The opinion of the Advocate General Szpunar of 22 February 2018 in the CJEU case of *Oberle*[175] covers numbers of interesting issues (mainly dealt with in chapter 12), and at Footnote 27 sets out:

> "It is also worth bearing in mind that Regulation No 650/2012 did not supplant — according to Article 75(1) thereof — bilateral conventions which were concluded with third countries before the date on which that regulation was adopted. Relatively often those conventions demarcate their scope on the basis of facts relating to the heir's nationality. This means that an authority of a Member State which is bound by those conventions will apply the conflict of laws rules and the rules of jurisdiction contained therein to situations falling within their scope. The application of those rules may lead to solutions which are incompatible with those resulting from the application of the rules of Regulation No 650/2012."

---

[174] In the case of OP C-21/22 considered below.

[175] C-20/17

Thus, it is clear that those Member States that have ratified international succession treaties will continue to be bound by them, save in relation to treaties solely between participating Member States or in relation to HCCH 11 (the Wills Convention, dealt with in chapter 15) or the Nordic Convention of 19 November 1934.

The Netherlands denounced its ratification of HccH 32, the Succession Convention, with effect from April 1, 2015, and HccH 32 is therefore no longer relevant for art.75. Czechia, Portugal and Slovakia have not denounced their ratification of HccH 21, the Estate Administration Convention, but since HccH 21 only creates an international certificate, its effects are unlikely to conflict directly with the Regulation.

Many EU Member States are subject to such treaties that, by virtue of art.75, are not affected by the Regulation.

Whilst many practitioners have, become more accustomed to the workings of the Regulation and the decisions of the CJEU on various Regulation aspects, very few have any direct experience of these EU/third State treaties. Indeed, finding an authoritative list of such treaties is nigh impossible.

Some of these relevant treaties that Member States have with third States are those that:

- Germany has with Iran (made in 1929), Russia and other USSR succession states (made 1958) and Turkey (made 1929),
- Austria has with Iran (made 1966) and Russia and other USSR succession states (made 1958),
- Italy has with Turkey (made 1929)
- Estonia, Latvia and Lithuania have with Russia (1993) and Ukraine (1995) and others

- France has with Denmark (1742), Dominican Republic (1882), Iran (1885), Cambodia (1949), Tunisia (1957), Algeria (1962) and Togo (1963)

- Greece has with Switzerland (1927).

The effect of art.75.1 is that for cross border successions between these states, the Regulation will not apply and the treaty will continue to apply.

It is understood that all of these states use nationality as the connecting factor and all other than Iran are schismatic using the *lex situs* for immovable property.

Some treaties only deal with issues of applicable law, whilst others only deal with jurisdiction, others with both. The Turkish treaties include issues of jurisdiction and recognition and enforcement and the Baltic treaties include jurisdiction based on situs. Those dealing solely with recognition and enforcement do not usually conflict with the Regulation.

To the extent that Russians and nationals of other USSR succession states such as the Ukraine or Kazakhstan may have cross border estate planning issues, the importance of the treaties with Baltic states, Germany and Austria may cause particular difficulties. For example, the Latvian house of a Russian national, who dies intestate, resident in France will be subject to the jurisdiction of the French courts and French law under the EU Succession Regulation, but Latvian jurisdiction and Russian law under the 1993 treaty as between Latvia and the USSS. It is not clear as to how this conflict is to be resolved. It is presumed that the French courts will have universal jurisdiction (but excluding the house in Latvia). A European Certificate of Succession issued in France ought to note the exclusion of the Latvian house in accordance with the 1993 treaty and that Russian law would apply to it.[176]

---

[176] The CJEU case of *E.E.* C-80/19 is an example of these issues.

Second generation Turks living in Germany or Italy or Iranians in Germany or Austria, may have difficulty in establishing which is their effective nationality, but this may mean that the relevant treaty is not applicable.

The differences of view from each end of the Italy/Swiss treaty are interesting. On the face of it, Article.17 of the 1868 Treaty, only deals with jurisdiction and states that succession disputes of an Italian are to be brought in the Italian courts and vice versa for Swiss citizens. It is not clear as to whether disputes include claims brought by creditors. In the Italian courts, creditors have succeeded in bringing such claims. On a separate issue, the Swiss courts have interpreted Article 17 as including an implied applicable law provision, whilst the Italian courts may not. The view of the CJEU, is likely to interpret the treaty narrowly, in order to ensure that the Regulation is only limited strictly as far as necessary.

The uncertainties of the French position ask as many questions as they answer. The definition of personal law in France does not include succession whilst elsewhere it usually does. It is therefore uncertain as to how the French treaties that do not specifically include references to succession be interpreted. The French position may be that it is only the 1957 Treaty with Tunisia, which specifically includes succession within the definition of personal status, that will override the Regulation for French purposes. Whilst traditionally in relation to its African colonies, succession was included in the definition of personal status, and still is in relation to the PIL of most of those colonies since independence, in practice, there does not seem to be any evidence of any treaties having an effect on succession in the French courts. The same issue applies to the 1964 French Treaty with Iran. The bulk of the Iran treaty applies to navigation and does not seem to have been applied to succession cases in either France or Iran in practice. This all leaves a very uncertain position in France, particularly since it seems to have been very much ignored.

The particular historical reasons for the concluding of these 20th Century treaties is of interest. The circumstances now, however, are somewhat different. Until Austria, Estonia, France, Germany, Italy, Latvia and

Lithuania can renegotiate these treaties, they will cause confusion and difficulty.

The history of the conventions with the Persian Empire after the abandonment of the doctrine of capitulation, by the great powers after the First World War, explains much. Also, the reality is that third States are unlikely to look favourably on any attempts to change or amend these historic treaties (and may well interpret them more broadly), leaving the EU to face the fact, that it cannot impose its will outside its own boundaries.

The CJEU case of *Anikovi*[177] dealt with in chapter 20, although dealing with interplay between Treaties and the Brussels II *ter* Regulation rather than the Succession Regulation is still of interest.

Brussels II *ter* has no specific Article dealing with existing treaties but its recital 91 states that, 'for agreements with one or more third States concluded by a Member State before the date of its accession to the Union, Article 351 TFEU applies'.

Article 351 TFEU states that "The rights and obligations arising from agreements concluded before 1 January 1958 or, for acceding States, before the date of their accession, between one or more Member States on the one hand, and one or more third countries on the other, shall not be affected by the provisions of the Treaties.

To the extent that such agreements are not compatible with the Treaties, the Member State or States concerned shall take all appropriate steps to eliminate the incompatibilities established. Member States shall, where necessary, assist each other to this end and shall, where appropriate, adopt a common attitude."

In this case, CJEU decided that if the provisions of the treaty are incompatible withBrussels II *ter*, and that incompatibility cannot be

[177] C-395/23

avoided by a court of that Member State in proceedings pending before it in a matter that is governed by both that treaty and that regulation, that court may apply the rules of that treaty to the detriment of those laid down by that regulation, as long as the measures necessary to eliminate that incompatibility have not taken effect, it being specified that that Member State must take all appropriate steps to adopt and implement those measures.

The CJEU case of *OP*[178] is directly on the Regulation and deals with the facts first referred to the CJEU in the case of *OKR.*[179]

Article 37 of the Treaty of 24 May 1993 between Poland and Ukraine on legal assistance and legal relations in civil and criminal matters provides that 'Legal relationships in matters relating to the succession of movable property shall be governed by the law of the contracting party of which the deceased was a national at the time of his or her death. Legal relationships in matters relating to the succession of immovable property shall be governed by the law of the contracting party in the territory of which that property is situated.

The classification of the property forming part of the estate as movable or immovable property shall be governed by the law of the contracting party in the territory of which the property is situated.'

Could a Ukrainian national habitually resident in Poland choose the succession law of Ukraine to apply to their Polish immovables?

CJEU made it clear that although art.22 must be interpreted as meaning that a third State national residing in a Member State may choose the law of that third State as the law governing his or her succession as a whole, art. 75, read in conjunction with art.22 must be interpreted as not precluding – where a Member State of the European Union has

178 C-21/22

179 C-387/20

concluded, before the adoption of that regulation, a bilateral agreement with a third State which designates the law applicable to succession and does not expressly provide for the possibility of choosing another law – a national of that third State, residing in the Member State in question, from not being able to choose the law of that third State to govern his or her succession as a whole.

Sadly, neither in the opinion of the AG Campos Sánchez-Bordona nor in the judgment of the court, was there any consideration as to the extended scope of the Regulation which may be wider than the definition of succession in a particular treaty. It could well be argued, that the decision of CJEU in this case does not prevent the exercise of a *professio juris,* but that its effects would be limited by the provisions of a Treaty.

It has been suggested that it would be helpful if the Commission were able to require Member States to notify the details of all relevant treaties and involve the Commission in any subsequent negotiations as under regulation (EU) No 1219/2012 of 12 December 2012 establishing transitional arrangements for bilateral investment agreements between Member States and third countries.

UK Belgian Treaty of 1934

The only treaty that is relevant for the United Kingdom is that of 2 May 1934 with Belgium. Under article 2, judgments pronounced in one state are recognised and enforced in the other, subject to various conditions. The convention specifically applies to succession matters, although under article 4(3)(b) "the jurisdiction of the original court shall be recognised in all cases where such recognition is in accordance with the rules of Private International Law observed by the court applied to." Decisions of United Kingdom courts will now be subject to recognition in Belgium being in accordance with the Regulation as the rules of private international law now applicable in Belgium. This has now affected the application of the treaty.

Article 11 enables the United Kingdom to extend the convention to crown dependencies or territories under UK suzerainty.

A cross-border estate involving connecting factors in a European Union member state subject to the Regulation and in a third State with a relevant treaty should immediately ring alarm bells. Deep thought will be required.

CHAPTER TWENTY-FOUR

PUBLIC POLICY

In civil law states, the doctrine of *ordre public* is designed to ensure that public welfare prevails, whereas, in common law states, matters of public policy such as fundamental rules of justice, human rights, morality or the interests of the state may override foreign law that would otherwise apply.

Article 35 follows similar restrictions in most EU regulations that the application of the provision of the law "specified by the Regulation may be refused only if such application is manifestly incompatible with the public policy (*ordre public)* of the forum".

Thus, it is only a specific provision that can be refused rather than the foreign law as a whole. The application of a provision of law can only be refused if it is manifestly incompatible with the public policy of the forum.

The initial draft regulation art.27.2 stating that the application of a rule is not to be contrary to public policy of the forum "on the sole ground that its clauses regarding the reserved portion of an estate differ from those in force in the forum" was removed, but recital 38 refers to this issue, although obliquely, "This Regulation should enable citizens to organise their succession in advance by choosing the law applicable to their succession. That choice should be limited to the law of a State of their nationality in order to ensure a connection between the deceased and the law chosen and to avoid a law being chosen with the intention of frustrating the legitimate expectations of persons entitled to a reserved share."

The Regulation makes it clear that the classification of a provision as being contrary to public policy is a matter for the forum and not a matter for the applicable succession law. Recital 58 limits the application of public policy refusal by stating that art.35 should only be applied in exceptional circumstances, and that the public-policy exception should not apply "in order to set aside the law of another State or to refuse to recognise or, as the case may be, accept or enforce a decision, an authentic instrument or a court settlement from another Member State when doing so would be contrary to the Charter of Fundamental Rights of the European Union, and in particular Article 21 thereof, which prohibits all forms of discrimination."

However, although the classification of a provision being contrary to public policy is a matter for the forum, the "concept of 'public policy' in the EU, particularly as justification for a derogation from the fundamental principles.., must be interpreted strictly, so that its scope cannot be determined unilaterally by each Member State without any control by the Community institutions. Thus, public policy may be relied on only if there is a genuine and sufficiently serious threat to a fundamental interest of society".[180] Although it will be a matter for the forum as to whether a provision is incompatible with public policy, it will be a matter for the CJEU as to what matters are within an EU wide definition of public policy limits.[181] As highlighted by recital 58, it would seem probable that the CJEU would in due course find against a decision of the courts of a Member State, if it expressed the view that the succession law of another Member State would not be recognised and enforced. Cultural norms do vary considerably and there is nothing to prevent the courts of a Member State finding that a particular provision of the law of another Member State is in breach of public policy.

Indeed, recent public policy exemption developments in France and Germany undermine the integrity of the Regulation, creating confusion and uncertainty for practitioners advising those with connections to Member States.

---

180 C-36/02, para. 30.

181 C-7/98, para. 23.

Le Droit de Prélèvement Compensatoire ("*prévélement*")

The concept of forced heirship, and particularly the protection from disinheritance enjoyed by the children of the deceased, known as the "*réserve héréditaire*", is a sacred and fundamental tenet of French succession law. That said, the limit on testamentary freedom has, more recently, been the subject of controversy in France.[182] In 2019, the French Ministry of Justice set a up a working group, the object of which was to explore options for restricting the reach of the *réserve*.[183] This exercise somewhat backfired because, instead, the working group firmly concluded that the *réserve* should stay. The view was that it remains the cornerstone of French inheritance law, aimed at realising the revolutionary ideal of equality amongst family and citizens, and that it should be protected on the international stage from the threat of influence from common law jurisdictions in which no such protection exists. It is against this backdrop that a right of compensatory levy for heirs that many believed had been long since consigned to history was reintroduced in France.[184]

Following the proposals put forward by the working group, in July 2021 the French Assemblée Nationale approved a draft bill aimed at reinforcing respect for the principles of the Republic.[185] Under the heading "Provisions relative to respect for human rights and to equality between men and women" was a proposal to amend Article 913 of the French civil code and reintroduce an old right of levy known as the "*Prélèvement*". The *Prélèvement* provides the children of the deceased with a right of compensation where they are disinherited by the

[182] S. El Haïry et N. Moutchou, *La philanthropie à la française*, rapport remis au premier Ministre, Feb. 2020, proposition No. 10.

[183] N. Belloubet, "Lettre de Mission", *Rapport du Groupe de Travail. La reserve heriditaire*, 28 Mara 2019.

[184] Rapport du Groupe de Travail, la Réserve héréditaire, remis le 13 decembre 2019.

[185] Bill No. 3649, December 2020, Respect des principes de la République.

application of a foreign law with no equivalent forced heirship rules. The explanatory memorandum accompanying the bill suggests that the objective of the *Prélèvement* was to ensure parity of treatment between men and women where the application of Shariah Law would see distinctions in the treatment of heirs based on gender. It's perhaps unsurprising that, even at the draft stage, the proposed amendment to Article 913 was criticised for failing to meet this objective for two reasons: firstly, because discrimination as between heirs based on characteristics like gender is contrary to the French *ordre public* in any event, and Article 913 offers no more protection than that already available under current French law; and secondly, because Muslim inheritance laws protect (both male and female) heirs from disinheritance and the *Prélèvement* therefore would not apply in such cases.[186] It has been suggested that the provision had another goal: to ensure the disregard of all foreign laws lacking an equivalent *Réserve.*[187]

The French right of *Prélèvement* is not new. It was previously in force under article 2 of *la loi du 14 juillet 1819* in terms of which French nationals had a right of compensation over French situs assets of a French deceased where their right to the *Réserve* was jettisoned under application of a foreign law. This earlier iteration of the *Prélèvement* was deemed unconstitutional by the French *Conseil constitutionnel* on 5 August 2011[188] because it contravened the principle of equality by virtue of extending only to French nationals.

The new law which came into force on 1 November 2021 goes some way to addressing this by extending the *Prélèvement* to all estates where the deceased or one of the heirs is either a national or habitually resident in *any* Member State. Given the globalised world we now inhabit, it is not

---

186 *An examination of the European and Constitutional Requirements of the Compensatory Levy in Draft Article 913 of the French Civil Code* By Suzel Ramaciotti, translation by Lily B. Teague

187 *ibid*

188 Decision no 2011-159 QPC du 5 août 2011 Mme Elke B, et autres

difficult to imagine that many foreigners with interests in France will be affected by article 913. The *Prélèvement* only applies where there is no forced heirship equivalent (protecting children) under the applicable foreign law. For those nationals of common law jurisdictions like England and Wales, who enjoy almost complete testamentary freedom, the consequences are serious. Given its limitations, lack of universality, and questions (already discussed in chapter 22) around whether it applies in estates of a non-domiciled deceased, it is unlikely that French courts would treat the protection available to the deceased's children under the Inheritance (Provision for Family and Dependents) Act 1975 as equivalent to the *Réserve*. British nationals previously able to avoid the application of the stringent *Réserve* and bequeath their French estate freely by making a choice of law election in favour of the law of England and Wales, could now face the full force of the *Prélèvement*.

The fact that the *Prélèvement* is limited to cases where the foreign law does not have any *Réserve* equivalent suggests that a choice of law election in favour of the law of Scotland might shelter a Scottish testator from its impact. The reference in Article 913 to "*aucun mechanism réservataire protecteur des enfants*"[189] or "no reserve mechanism protecting children" suggests that the mere existence of the indefeasible, albeit limited, protection for children under Scottish legal rights is sufficient to defeat the *Prélèvement*. Whether French courts will agree remains to be seen.

Now that many citizens have acquired multiple nationalities in order to retain their rights as EU citizens, other laws may come into account. Many UK citizens have Irish nationality and may choose Irish law in order to enable a choice of Ireland as a jurisdiction. It is presumed that the succession rights under the Succession Act 1965 which do not give rights to children, would not give shelter to the impact of Article 913.

Is the *Prélèvement* compatible with the Regulation?

---

[189] Article 913, alinea 3, code civil français

Since the introduction of the *Prélèvement* the welcome legal certainty provided under the Regulation, and enjoyed by those with interests in France, has been lost. Critics suggest that by making a change to its own substantive private international law, rather than invoking a public policy exception, the *Prélèvement* cannot be compatible with the Regulation because of the universality of the applicable law under art.20. [190] France can only look to the Regulation for deaths after 17 August 2015 and there is no provision in the Regulation that allows a Member State to apply its own substantive international law.[191] The applicable law is either the law of the deceased's last habitual residence (art. 21) or the law of the deceased's nationality if a valid choice of law has been made (art. 22). Further, art.23 tells us that the applicable law under the regulation "will govern the succession as a whole" and then goes on to list specific matters that are governed "in particular" by the applicable law thereby suggesting that the list is not exhaustive.[192]

As discussed more fully in chapter 7, there is an exception to the general applicable law rule under art.30 of the Regulation, which allows the use of local inheritance laws that place restrictions on the succession of certain categories of assets for economic, family or social considerations. Recital 54 makes clear that the scope of this exception is limited and, specifically, that "provisions providing for a reserved share of the estate greater than that provided for in the law applicable to the succession" cannot "be regarded as constituting special rules imposing restrictions concerning or affecting the succession in respect of certain assets".

If French law is not applicable to the succession as a whole, the "*Prélèvement*" does not apply and it would appear that the only option available to protect the forced heirship rights of children in France would

---

190 Which method? Right of levy, the "*reserve héréditaire*" and protection of heirs against discrimination by Nathalie Joubert, translation by Lily B. Teague

191 Ibid

192 See Chapter 7, *Applicable Law – Chapter III of the Regulation*

be to invoke the public policy exception under art. 35.[193] However, as discussed in the introductory paragraphs to this chapter, while the classification of a provision as contrary to public policy is a matter for the forum, it will be for the CJEU to decide which matters are within an EU wide definition of public policy limits[194] and recital 58 makes clear that the CJEU would allow a public policy exception only in "exceptional" circumstances. It has been suggested by some commentators that European legislators envisaged sufficient protection of the *Réserve* by designation of the applicable law as the deceased's last habitual residence and restriction of a choice of law to the law of the deceased's nationality which, in accordance with recital 38, is "to ensure a connection between the deceased and the law chosen and to avoid a law being chosen with the intention of frustrating the legitimate expectations of persons entitled to a reserved share".[195]

The working group instructed to explore the application of the reserve in 2019 recommended that the *Réserve* should be recognised as a matter of international public policy insofar as it belongs to the principles relating to the political, family and social foundations of society.[196] In a ministerial response to a question on "*succession international et la part réservataire*" the French ministry of justice explains that the reintroduction of the *Prélèvement* makes forced heirship a principle of French public policy and that Article 913 is therefore "within the scope of art. 35" of the Regulation.[197]

---

193 Which method? Right of levy, the "*réserve héréditaire*" and protection of heirs against discrimination by Nathalie Joubert, translation by Lily B. Teague

194 C-7/98, para. 23.

195 Which method? Right of levy, the "*réserve héréditaire*" and protection of heirs against discrimination by Nathalie Joubert, translation by Lily B. Teague

196 Rapport du Groupe de Travail, la Réserve héréditaire, remis le 13 decembre 2019

197 Question n°7936 : Succession internationale et part réservataire -

The ministerial response specifically references the 2017 decision of the French Cour de Cassation in *Jarre* clarifying that the reintroduction of Article 913 reverses the Court's jurisprudence by making the reserve a "principle of international public policy". The case centred on the death of Maurice Jarre who died on 29 March 2009 having lived in California for over 40 years leaving his estate to his then spouse using a US trust. His children from a previous relationship, Stéphanie and Jean-Michel Jarre claimed that they were entitled to a share of his estate. The Cour de Cassation concluded that the designation of a foreign law that ignores the *Réserve* can only be rejected "*if it leads to a situation incompatible with principles of French law considered essential*" and that "*to the extent that the claimants are not in a situation of economic precariousness or need, there is no reason to disregard the conflicts rule*".

Following the judgement of the Cour de Cassation, Stéphanie and Jean-Michel took their case to the ECtHR[198] arguing that they had been prejudiced by the *Prélèvement's* fleeting absence from 2011 when it was abolished and 2021 when it was reintroduced under Article 913 of the French civil code.

European Court of Human Rights (ECtHR)

The ECtHR upheld the 2017 judgement of the French Cour de Cassation stating that the ECtHR "has never recognised the existence of the general and unconditional right of children to inherit part of their parents' property". The judgement of the ECtHR may provide some helpful insight into how art.35 might be interpreted by the CJEU.[199]

Assemblée nationale

198 *Jarre v France* n° 14157/18 ECtHR 15 February 2024

199 *Forced Heirship is not a Human Right,* Patrick Delas [2024] P.C.B., Issue 3

The future of the *Prélèvement*

While several complaints have been made to the European Commission about Article 913 of the French civil code and its perceived lack of compatibility with the Regulation, it will take a decision of the CJEU to put the question beyond doubt. In the aftermath of Brexit and given more recent political developments across the European continent, it's conceivable that the CJEU may be cautious of interfering with the autonomy of individual Member States, especially in relation to the applicable laws of the parts of the UK and other third states that do not have similar succession rights to those of Member States. Only time will tell.

Case no. IV ZR 110/21

Like France, Germany has also resisted the application of the Regulation where it was deemed incompatible with the fundamental principles of German succession law. On 29 June 2022 in *Case no. IV ZR 110/21* the *Bundesgerichtshof* upheld an earlier decision of the Cologne Court of Appeal[200] that the application of English law to the succession of a UK national residing in Germany violated the German *ordre public*. The case involved an English testator who had lived in Germany for over 50 years. He had made a choice of law election under art. 22 in favour of English law as the law to govern the succession to his estate as a whole. The plaintiff in the case was the testator's adopted son (and a German national). Having been excluded from benefiting from the estate in his father's will, the plaintiff requested information relative to the estate and claimed the compulsory portion he was entitled to, by virtue of his being a child of the testator, under German succession law.

Having confirmed that the testator was able to elect English law as the law applicable to his estate as a whole under art.22, the court then

[200] Case no. 24 U 77/20

considered the question of whether the application of English law in the circumstances of this particular case constituted a violation of German public policy such that the art. 35 exception was validly invoked. It concluded that "*the application of English law is, at least in the case at issue here, obviously incompatible with the German ordre public.... This is because English law is in such serious contraction with the distribution of the estate constitutionally guaranteed under German Law that its application in the case here is unacceptable. This has the consequence that it does not apply here.*" The court referenced Articles 14 (1) and 6 (1) of the German Constitution[201] which, according to a significant decision by the German Federal Constitutional Court (the Bundesvergassungsgericht) in 2005,[202] guarantees the right of children to the compulsory portion in the estate of a deceased parent irrespective of need. The court held that this right was protected by virtue of the sanctity of the relationship between parent and child. There was, according to the Bundesgerichtshof, no equivalent protection under English law. The court took the view that the right to claim financial provision afforded to children under the Inheritance (Provision for Family and Dependants) Act 1975 was not comparable to the guarantee enjoyed by them under German succession law. This view was taken because the right is discretionary in nature and only available where the deceased died domiciled in England and Wales and so would not have been available in this case.

What does the decision in Case no. IV ZR 110/21 mean for the future of the Regulation?

Germany has done what France has not and has invoked the art. 35 exception on the basis that, in this particular case, the application of English law was "manifestly incompatible" with German *ordre public.* While, on the face of it, the *Bundesgerichtshof's* decision appears to fly in

201 Grundgesetz für die Bundesrepublik Deutschland

202 BVerG, Order of the First Senate of 19 April 2005 – 1 BvR 1644/00-, paras. 1-98

the face of the principles of the Regulation, the court, rather than adopt a blanket approach, placed considerable emphasis on the circumstances of this case such that it's future impact may be limited. Both the deceased and his adopted son had strong ties to Germany. While the *Bundesgerichtshof* placed significant emphasis on the strength of the deceased's and his son's "domestic connections" to Germany, unhelpfully, no definition of what constitutes a domestic connection strong enough to justify invoking art. 35 was provided. Consideration was given to the habitual residence of the deceased and his son, both in the years leading up to, and at the time of the testator's death; the fact that the testator's assets were situated in Germany; and the son's German nationality.

The decision of the *Bundesgerichtshof* is at odds with the French decision in *Jarre* as well as those of other European jurisdictions in which the courts concerned concluded that the application of a foreign law that ignores domestic rights of forced heirship is not incompatible with the *ordre public.*[203] For this reason, and because it is for the CJEU to "*monitor the outer limits within which a state may rely on the ordre public in the first place due to the embedding of the ordre public*" in art. 35, commentators have suggested that a referral to the CJEU would have been helpful.[204]

While it is impossible to make predictions about the reach of the consequences of this jurisprudence in the future, it has created unwelcome uncertainty for those with connections to Germany. The art. 35 exception may apply even if the foreign law does not completely exclude the beneficiary entitled to the compulsory portion but falls short

203 See decisions of Oberster Gerichtshof OGH Vienna, judgement of 25 February 2021, case number 2 Ob 214/20i; and Corte suprema di cassazione, Rome, judgement of 24 June 1996, Case no. 5832

204 Infringement of English inheritance law against German ordre public due to the absence of a right to a compulsory portion of children – discussion of BGH, judgement of 29 June 2022 – IV ZR 110/21 by lawyer, Dr Axel Wenzel and lawyer David Falkowski, Cologne.

of what they would be entitled to in Germany.[205] It seems clear from this decision that the *Bundesgerichtshof* will not look favourably on financial provisions like those available under the Inheritance (Provisions for Family and Dependants) Act 1975 which are discretionary in nature and available depending on the economic circumstances of the claimant. Given the emphasis placed by the court on the need for a "domestic connection", those with fewer significant ties to Germany may be able to avoid the impact of the compulsory portion by making an election under art. 22. However, the lack of clarity around the strength of domestic connection needed to invoke an art. 35 exception means that any testator with any links to Germany should exercise caution around their succession plans.

Application of Public Policy

Art. 35 is silent as to what happens if a public policy exception is validly applied to a particular foreign law provision and as to what provision is then to be inserted in its place. It is likely that the courts will normally wish to apply the appropriate provision of the law of the forum (and this was the approach taken by the *Bundesegerichtshof* in Case no. IV ZR 110/21). However, this may not necessarily be the most appropriate. Such a foreign law provision is not outside the scope of the Regulation, so that it could be argued that it is disapplied, another provision of the foreign law should then be applied and that there is no discretion to apply the law of the forum in any event.

---

205 *Ibid*

CHAPTER TWENTY-FIVE

FUTURE DEVELOPMENTS AND CONCLUSIONS

EU law is not static and is generally subject to review. The Brussels I and Brussels II regulations in particular have been subject to amendment over the years. The Regulation is no exception and art.82 sets out that the Commission is to report on the Regulation in August 2025 with an evaluation of any practical problems on out of court settlements and with proposals for amendments to the Regulation. The European Law Institute has been looking at the principles of extra-judicial administration of justice in cross-border family and succession matters.[206]

Will Registers

There are no articles in the Regulation on the topic of Will Registers. The Council of Ministers invited the Commission to launch preparatory work in relation to an electronic register of European Certificates of Succession.

The Commission project "Further developments in the area of interconnection of registers of wills", focused in 2014-2016 on the possibility of making cross-border succession more efficient by electronic means, led by Estonia and carried out in cooperation with the European Network of Registers of Wills Association (ENRWA)/Association du Réseau Européen des Registres Testamentaires (ARERT)[207] and the

---

[206] https://europeanlawinstitute.eu/projects-publications/current-projects/current-projects/eli-principles-extra-judicial-administration-of-justice-in-cross-border-family-and-succession-matters/

[207] http://www.arert.eu/?lang=en

Council of the Notariats of the EU (CNUE). It recommended that EU Member States should implement cross-border electronic information, data and document exchange.[208] This subject is likely to be subject to further consideration and development.

Changes to Succession Rights

As highlighted in chapter 3, succession rights and law continue to develop in each Member State. Inheritance contracts are now available under systems that previously did not accept them. The bite of clawback may diminish in favour of maintenance needs and the signs are that party autonomy and *professio juris* are also being considered more widely. Switzerland has changed its PIL with effect from 1 January 2025[209] to take into account the Regulation and other third States may well consider doing so too.

Taxation

Whilst capital and estate taxation, and the application of freedom of movement to it is outside the scope of the Regulation, the CJEU has been active on the subject and the two areas of succession and its taxation may overlap in the future. The EU Commission produced a recommendation in 2011 with a view to reducing multiple inheritance taxation in the EU.[210] This has had no take up or effect as of yet but the report of the experts[211] is helpful.

---

208 Accessible via e-justice https://beta.e-justice.europa.eu/166/EN/succession

209 FF 2024 32 - Loi fédérale sur le droit internati... | Fedlex

210 2011/856/EU https://ec.europa.eu/taxation_customs/sites/taxation/files/resources/documents/taxation/personal_tax/inheritance/c_2011_8819_en.pdf

211 Available at https://op.europa.eu/en/publication-detail/-/publication/faa0871d-ca40-11e5-a4b5-01aa75ed71a1

Future

It is highly unlikely that any other state joining the EU would be permitted to opt out of the Regulation and therefore its reach is likely to increase in the future.

It will be interesting to see the results of the review of the Regulation to begin in 2025 and what changes, if any may be proposed.

To what extent may the limits that national courts place around the Regulation under the grounds of public policy or otherwise, erode its usefulness and how may the EU Institutions react.

Cross border estates and the Regulation are not only here to stay, but their influence is growing. Habitual Residence is not only the connecting factor for EU legislation but also of HccH conventions. The more that is known of the procedures and laws of other systems, the more influence that they will have. National jurisdictional boundaries will diminish in the EU. Digital assets highlight the difficulty in distinguishing between assets and access to those assets. As the world becomes ever more virtual, cross border issues will intensify and access will be key.

APPENDIX

RESOURCES

https://beta.e-justice.europa.eu/517/EN/inheritance

https://europa.eu/youreurope/citizens/family/inheritances/planning-inheritance/index_en.htm

http://www.successions-europe.eu

http://www.arert.eu/?lang=en

http://www.arert.eu/Information-sheets.html?lang=fr

INDEX

MORE BOOKS BY LAW BRIEF PUBLISHING

A selection of our other titles available now:-

'A Practical Guide to Probation Breaches and Other Applications' by Mark Thomas
'A Practical Guide to Remarriage and Divorce' by Cordelia Williams & Claire Howard
'A Practical Guide to Privacy, Transparency, Reporting Restrictions and Closed Proceedings in the Court of Protection' by Laura Mannering
'Beaumont on Barristers – A Guide to Defending Disciplinary Proceedings (Second Edition)' by Marc Beaumont
'A Practical Guide to Payments for Environmental Services' by Ben Sharples
'A Practical Guide to the Law of Pregnancy and Maternity at Work' by Rebecca Thomas
'A Practical Guide to Redundancy – Second Edition' by Philip Hyland & Collette Moore
'A Practical Guide to International Issues for Scottish Family Lawyers' by Susie Mountain, Donna McKay, Ken MacDonald
'A Practical Guide to the Law on Deprivation of Liberty' by Ben Troke
'A Practical Guide to Rights over Airspace and Subsoil – Second Edition' by Daniel Gatty
'A Practical Guide to the Law in Relation to Inquests' by Ramya Nagesh
'A Practical Guide to the Construction and Rectification of Wills and Trust Instruments (Second Edition)' by Edward Hewitt
'A Practical Guide to Data Protection in Social Housing' by Clare Paterson
'A Practical Guide to Spousal Maintenance – Second Edition' by Liz Cowell
'A Practical Guide to International Parental Child Abduction Law (England and Wales)' by Dr Onyója Momoh
'A Practical Guide to Deprivation of British Citizenship' by Sean Ell
'A Practical Guide to Commercial Property Service Charges' by Rachel Garton
'A Practical Guide to Clinical Negligence – Third Edition' by Geoffrey Simpson-Scott (Geoff)
'A Practical Guide to the Rights of Grandparents in Children Proceedings – Second Edition' by Stuart Barlow

'The Electronic Communications Code: A Practical Guide – Second Edition' by Kerry Bretherton KC, James Castle, Mark Loveday
'A Practical Guide to the Independent School Standards – September 2023 Edition' by Sarah McKimm
'A Practical Guide to Estate Administration and Crypto Assets' by Richard Marshall
'A Practical Guide to Parental Alienation in Private and Public Law Children Cases' by Sam King QC & Frankie Shama
'Contested Heritage – Removing Art from Land and Historic Buildings' by Richard Harwood QC, Catherine Dobson, David Sawtell
'The Limits of Separate Legal Personality: When Those Running a Company Can Be Held Personally Liable for Losses Caused to Third Parties Outside of the Company' by Dr Mike Wilkinson
'A Practical Guide to Transgender Law' by Robin Moira White & Nicola Newbegin
'A Practical Guide to 'Stranded Spouses' in Family Law' by Mani Singh Basi
'A Practical Guide to Residential Freehold Conveyancing' by Lorraine Richardson
'A Practical Guide to Pensions on Divorce for Lawyers' by Bryan Scant
'A Practical Guide to Challenging Sham Marriage Allegations in Immigration Law' by Priya Solanki
'A Practical Guide to Digital Communications Evidence in Criminal Law' by Sam Willis
'A Practical Guide to Legal Rights in Scotland' by Sarah-Jane Macdonald
'A Practical Guide to New Build Conveyancing' by Paul Sams & Rebecca East
'A Practical Guide to Inherited Wealth on Divorce' by Hayley Trim
'A Practical Guide to Practice Direction 12J and Domestic Abuse in Private Law Children Proceedings' by Rebecca Cross & Malvika Jaganmohan
'A Practical Guide to Confiscation and Restraint' by Narita Bahra QC, John Carl Townsend, David Winch
'A Practical Guide to the Law of Forests in Scotland' by Philip Buchan
'A Practical Guide to Health and Medical Cases in Immigration Law' by Rebecca Chapman & Miranda Butler
'A Practical Guide to Bad Character Evidence for Criminal Practitioners by Aparna Rao
'A Practical Guide to Extradition Law post-Brexit' by Myles Grandison et al
'A Practical Guide to Hoarding and Mental Health for Housing Lawyers' by Rachel Coyle

'Stephens on Contractual Indemnities' by Richard Stephens
'A Practical Guide to the EU Succession Regulation' by Richard Frimston
'A Practical Guide to Solicitor and Client Costs – Second Edition' by Robin Dunne
'Constructive Dismissal – Practice Pointers and Principles' by Benjimin Burgher
'A Practical Guide to Religion and Belief Discrimination Claims in the Workplace' by Kashif Ali
'A Practical Guide to the Law of Medical Treatment Decisions' by Ben Troke
'Fundamental Dishonesty and QOCS in Personal Injury Proceedings: Law and Practice' by Jake Rowley
'A Practical Guide to the Law in Relation to School Exclusions' by Charlotte Hadfield & Alice de Coverley
'A Practical Guide to Divorce for the Silver Separators' by Karin Walker
'The Right to be Forgotten – The Law and Practical Issues' by Melissa Stock
'A Practical Guide to Planning Law and Rights of Way in National Parks, the Broads and AONBs' by James Maurici QC, James Neill et al
'A Practical Guide to Election Law' by Tom Tabori
'A Practical Guide to the Law in Relation to Surrogacy' by Andrew Powell
'A Practical Guide to Claims Arising from Fatal Accidents – Second Edition' by James Patience
'A Practical Guide to Asbestos Claims' by Jonathan Owen & Gareth McAloon
'A Practical Guide to Stamp Duty Land Tax in England and Northern Ireland' by Suzanne O'Hara
'A Practical Guide to the Law of Farming Partnerships' by Philip Whitcomb
'A Practical Guide to the Law of Unlawful Eviction and Harassment – Second Edition' by Stephanie Lovegrove
'A Practical Guide to Costs in Personal Injury Claims – Second Edition' by Matthew Hoe
'A Practical Guide to the General Data Protection Regulation (GDPR) – Second Edition' by Keith Markham
'A Practical Guide to Working with Litigants in Person and McKenzie Friends in Family Cases' by Stuart Barlow
'Protecting Unregistered Brands: A Practical Guide to the Law of Passing Off' by Lorna Brazell
'A Practical Guide to Secondary Liability and Joint Enterprise Post-Jogee' by Joanne Cecil & James Mehigan

'A Practical Guide to the Pre-Action RTA Claims Protocol for Personal Injury Lawyers' by Antonia Ford
'A Practical Guide to Neighbour Disputes and the Law' by Alexander Walsh
'A Practical Guide to Coercive Control for Legal Practitioners and Victims' by Rachel Horman
'A Practical Guide to the Law of Driverless Cars – Second Edition'
by Alex Glassbrook, Emma Northey & Scarlett Milligan
'A Practical Guide to TOLATA Claims' by Greg Williams
'A Practical Guide to Elderly Law – Second Edition' by Justin Patten
'A Practical Guide to Responding to Housing Disrepair and Unfitness Claims' by Iain Wightwick
'A Practical Guide to the Law of Bullying and Harassment in the Workplace' by Philip Hyland
'How to Be a Freelance Solicitor: A Practical Guide to the SRA-Regulated Freelance Solicitor Model' by Paul Bennett
'A Practical Guide to Prison Injury Claims' by Malcolm Johnson
'A Practical Guide to Advising Clients at the Police Station' by Colin Stephen McKeown-Beaumont
'A Practical Guide to Antisocial Behaviour Injunctions – Second Edition' by Iain Wightwick
'Practical Mediation: A Guide for Mediators, Advocates, Advisers, Lawyers, and Students in Civil, Commercial, Business, Property, Workplace, and Employment Cases' by Jonathan Dingle with John Sephton
'The Mini-Pupillage Workbook' by David Boyle
'A Practical Guide to Crofting Law' by Brian Inkster
'A Practical Guide to the Law of Domain Names and Cybersquatting' by Andrew Clemson
'A Practical Guide to the Law of Gender Pay Gap Reporting' by Harini Iyengar
'NHS Whistleblowing and the Law' by Joseph England
'Employment Law and the Gig Economy' by Nigel Mackay & Annie Powell
'A Practical Guide to Noise Induced Hearing Loss (NIHL) Claims' by Andrew Mckie, Ian Skeate, Gareth McAloon
'An Introduction to Beauty Negligence Claims – A Practical Guide for the Personal Injury Practitioner' by Greg Almond
'Intercompany Agreements for Transfer Pricing Compliance' by Paul Sutton
'Zen and the Art of Mediation' by Martin Plowman
'A Practical Guide to Adoption for Family Lawyers' by Graham Pegg

‘A Practical Guide to Industrial Disease Claims’ by Andrew Mckie & Ian Skeate
‘A Practical Guide to Conducting a Sheriff Court Proof’ by Andrew Stevenson
‘A Practical Guide to Vicarious Liability’ by Mariel Irvine
‘A Practical Guide to Applications for Landlord’s Consent and Variation of Leases’ by Mark Shelton
‘A Practical Guide to Relief from Sanctions Post-Mitchell and Denton’ by Peter Causton
‘A Practical Guide to Equity Release for Advisors’ by Paul Sams
‘A Practical Guide to Financial Services Claims’ by Chris Hegarty
‘A Practical Guide to Financial Ombudsman Service Claims’ by Adam Temple & Robert Scrivenor
‘A Practical Guide to Running Housing Disrepair and Cavity Wall Claims – Second Edition’ by Andrew Mckie & Ian Skeate
‘A Practical Guide to Holiday Sickness Claims – Second Edition’ by Andrew Mckie & Ian Skeate
‘Arguments and Tactics for Personal Injury and Clinical Negligence Claims’ by Dorian Williams
‘A Practical Guide to Drone Law’ by Rufus Ballaster, Andrew Firman, Eleanor Clot
‘On Experts: CPR35 for Lawyers and Experts’ by David Boyle
‘An Introduction to Personal Injury Law’ by David Boyle

These books and more are available to order online direct from the publisher at www.lawbriefpublishing.com, where you can also read free sample chapters. For any queries, call us on 0844 587 2383 or email us at mail@lawbriefpublishing.com.

Our books are all generally in stock at www.amazon.co.uk with free next day delivery for Prime members, and at good legal bookshops such as Wildy & Sons.

We are regularly launching new books in our series of practical day-to-day practitioners' guides. Visit our website and join our free newsletter to be kept informed and to receive special offers, free chapters, etc.

You can also follow us on Twitter at www.twitter.com/lawbriefpub.

www.ingramcontent.com/pod-product-compliance
Ingram Content Group UK Ltd.
Pitfield, Milton Keynes, MK11 3LW, UK
UKHW020136290926
15471UKWH00003B/520

9 781914 608520